The
Student
Cookbook

The
Student
Cookbook

Miranda Shearer

First published in the United Kingdom in 2002 by
Cassell Illustrated, a division of Octopus Publishing Group Ltd

This edition published 2006 by Bounty Books,
a division of Octopus Publishing Group Ltd
2–4 Heron Quays, London E14 4JP

ISBN-13: 978-0-753714-35-5
ISBN-10: 0-753714-35-3

A CIP catalogue record for this book is available
from the British Library

Printed and bound in China

Contents

Introduction

Cooking for me is a totally unsure thing. You can follow a recipe down to the last 't' and the end result can still be disgusting, salty, burnt or look awful. It is about testing, trying, getting angry and frustrated. It can also be ego boosting and good fun. I find it incredible that you can start off with four or fifteen raw ingredients and chop them, mix them, watch them boil and change colour, burn, smell good and bad. Cooking is flexible when you feel confident; you can make it work for you, so don't be afraid of trial and error, or embarrassed if someone doesn't like your creation – just ask them for advice and experiment.

It was my mum's fault I became a so-called cook. I remember eating toast and honey one Sunday evening at the age of nine – a typical picture in my house, after yet another amazing Sunday lunch whipped up by mum who is able to have a bath, read half the papers or her book and talk to friends at the same time as roasting a loin of pork to feed the usual minimum of ten people she invites over. She casually said: 'You could do this, Miranda', so I did. I entered the 'Sainsbury's Future Cooks Competition' and got through 40,000 entrants to the regional finals. I had to cook two courses in front of five judges in 75 minutes. I was the youngest entrant that year and I don't know why, but I went back for more the following two years. It was hell. I remember screaming at my mother, crying over onions, running away, and my poor family having to eat the same meal every weekend for at least six weeks while I perfected it!

I don't even have amazing memories of the competitions, apart from my three brilliant godmothers making me feel like a star. The first year, the Lemon and Orange Fromage was overset with lumps of gelatine. The second year, I cooked the Banana Soufflé to perfection, but too early so one of the judges told me to keep it warm in the oven, and it sank lower than the *Titanic*.

There are certainly numerous occasions where things have not gone to plan, but it's like falling off a horse. Supposedly, the more times you fall, the more experienced you become. So here I am, in total shock that a few years on from my 'Future Cook' days, it actually came true and I am having a book published. This book was actually meant for just one person, but it's wicked that it will be used by many more. I am hoping it won't be just a Christmas stocking filler, which then gets slipped into a bag by mum while you are not looking, and is later used to roll a joint, or put at the back of a cupboard after accidentally falling in the washing-up bowl!

The main person I would like to thank for this success is my incredible mama, who has taught me everything I know, yet at the same time respects what I say about her food. She is the most amazing person and cooks the most scrumptious and original food. She always manages to rescue things that look like they are about to die – mine and hers. Her sixth sense for flavours and colours and everything you could possibly imagine to do with food will never be matched by anyone, and I want her to know she is my idol.

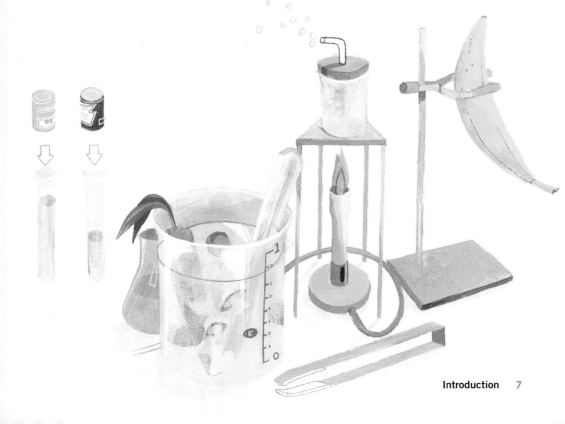

Before You Start

The obvious

- Read through the recipe to make sure you have everything you need.
- Collect all the ingredients together. Weigh dry ingredients; measure liquid ones in a measuring jug.
- Move oven shelves to the right position. Cook things on the middle shelf unless the recipe says something different. Switch on the oven to the given temperature, giving you time to prepare and the oven time to heat up.

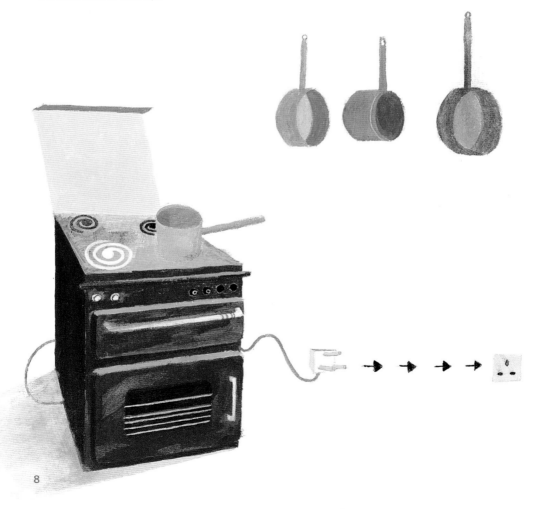

Myths and truths about what you are about to do

- Onions do make you cry, you can stop it by keeping the roots on while chopping. Some onions are stronger than others and need sautéing a bit longer.
- Washing vegetables is always good to do as they are either muddy or sprayed with chemicals.
- Peeling and seeding tomatoes is not to make cooking difficult – the skins are usually tough and the seeds make the food bitter. Boil some water, cross the bottoms of the tomatoes and drop them in for a few seconds, then take them out and they will be easy to peel.
- Smell food before you cook it – you can usually tell if it's rank unless you lose your sense of what smells good after a few years at uni!
- Tasting is always a good thing to do while cooking – just don't eat it all before it's ready or you will end up a fat pie muncher!
- Some of the recipes have herbs in and other bits and pieces that you can add or not, depending whether you have them or you are too lazy. After cooking for a while you can judge how much parsley or coriander or nutmeg to add, if you like it. **Just don't miss out a main ingredient, please!**
- Most leftovers, in fact all the ones I can think of, can be kept in the fridge (for no longer than a week!) and can be heated up in the microwave after a huge drinking session or for breakfast.

Measurements

- You can double, triple, quadruple or halve quantities to suit the number of people eating.

Things to remember

- Do not open the oven door while things are cooking.
- Turn off the oven when you have finished.

Cooking words

Bake	Cook food in an oven.
Beat	Mix by stirring vigorously with a fork, wooden spoon or whisk.
Blanch	Immerse, usually a vegetable, in boiling water for a minute or two.
Boil	Cook in boiling water.
Bring to the boil	Heat a liquid until it starts to boil.
Cream	Beat ingredients, often butter and sugar, together with a wooden spoon until creamy.
Curdle	This hapens when you beat something like butter, sugar and eggs together and they don't blend in (it sort of looks like sick!). You can usually fix it – if you're making a cake, adding the flour can help; if you're making mayonnaise, break a new egg into a clean bowl, start with the oil again then slowly add the curdled mixture.
Diced	Cut into small cubes like the ones used for maths in school.
Flour	There are two types of flour. Use plain flour unless otherwise specified; self-raising flour is usually for baking cakes or bread. And cornflour is used in very small quantities to thicken things. **Always sift flour to check for weevils**.
Fold in	Gently mix an ingredient into a creamed mixture using a **metal spoon** only.
Fry	Cook in hot fat or oil.
Garnish	Decorate food, often with herbs.
Glaze	Coat food with beaten egg, milk or melted jam to make it look glossy.
Grease	Rub a baking sheet, dish or cake tin with butter to stop food sticking.
Grill	Cook food under a grill.
Knead	Work a dough firmly with your hands on a flat surface until smooth and stretchy.
Marinade	A sauce in which you soak meat or fish to make it tender and give it flavour.
Rub in	Rub pieces of butter into flour with fingertips until mixture looks like breadcrumbs.
Sauté	Fry food in shallow oil or cook gently until soft and translucent, not brown. Can take between 2 and 30 minutes, depending on the recipe.
Season	Add salt, pepper, spices or herbs to food to give it more flavour. 'Season to taste' means add salt and pepper, then dip a finger in and taste – add more if you think it's lacking something.
Simmer	Cook a liquid over a low heat so that it is just bubbling, not boiling.
Whisk	Beat vigorously with a whisk to add air to a mixture and make it light.
Zest	Grate just the skin off the orange or lemon – not the white pith, which is bitter.

Cooking things

Tip: Much of this stuff can be found in car boot sales in the summer before you go to uni. Tom and I picked up some amazing bargains and equipped his kitchen quite cheaply.

Baking sheet/tray	Essential for grimy uni ovens, and for baking cookies.
Cake tin	Deep tin (usually round) to bake cakes in.
Chopping board	So you don't hack up the work surfaces.
Colander	To drain pasta and vegetables in (or to wear on your head at a mad party!).
Flan tin	A shallow tin with a frilly edge for quiches and tarts.
Frying pan	Like the one you used to use in races on pancake day.
Garlic press	If you're not keen on chunks of garlic in your food, spend some loose shrapnel on a garlic press. It's worth it for the flavour and is much easier than finely chopping it.
Grater	Box graters are the best, but mind your knuckles!
Knives	A few different sized ones are always useful.
Lemon squeezer	Useful for freshly squeezed orange juice, for breakfast in bed!
Measuring jug	To measure out fluids (such as alcohol for cocktails).
Metal slice	To look professional when serving your tarts and cakes.
Mixing bowl	To mix ingredients in – and always good to lick afterwards!
Ovenproof dish	A dish that you can use in the oven at high temperatures.
Palette knife	Not to mix oil paints with, but good for spreading mixtures like icing on a cake.
Pastry brush	Looks like a small paintbrush with softer bristles.
Pepper grinder	You can't beat freshly ground pepper – it's much nicer than the powdered stuff.
Potato peeler	Don't throw it away with the peel, easier and faster than a knife.
Rolling pin	Big long wooden thing the farmer's wife chases the farmer with.
Saucepan	Yes, there is a difference between this and a frying pan.
Scales	To weigh ingredients.
Scissors	Bigger and sharper than nail scissors.
Sieve	To sift flour, in case your flour is old and has weevils in.
Spatula	To scrape out bowls so you don't leave loads of mixture behind to eat.
Timer	If you don't buy one of these, I guarantee everything will burn.
Tin opener	Better not to wreck a knife (and your hands), so splash out on one of these.
Whisk	To beat mixtures with.
Wire rack	For cooling cakes, you can turn it into a BBQ in the summer.

Soups and Starters

Starters are important because they set the tone of the meal, and if you are hungry they are a good thing to have if you are waiting for the main course to cook. They should be light, and the helpings not too large.

Balance the first course with the dishes that are to follow. A simple salad thrown together can be way better than something rich that has taken hours to prepare. Crudités – chopped celery and carrot sticks with dips – work well. Croûtons – sliced and fried French bread – are great with soups.

Stock

To make soup you are going to need stock. You can use stock cubes, but I would personally kill you and it is a waste of chicken bones after a good roast. This recipe makes enough for at least one soup. If there isn't enough, add some more water or a dash of milk.

• Break up the bones of the chicken, duck or any other bird (not yours!), and put them in a big pan.
• Add 1 stick of celery, 1 or 2 peeled and halved carrots, depending on size. Add 1 onion with a clove stuck in it if you have one, 5 peppercorns, a bouquet of some parsley stalks tied with string, and the white bit of 1 leek. If you're feeling lazy, just onions and carrots are fine.
• Cover with about 2 litres cold water, add 1 teaspoon salt and bring to the boil, repeatedly skimming off the froth and scum with a spoon as it rises.
• When it is boiling, lower the heat and let the stock bubble very gently, uncovered, for about 3 hours.
•Allow to cool and then strain through a sieve. When cold put in the fridge or use immediately.

• For vegetable stock take 2 onions, 3 sticks of celery, 2 carrots, 1 fennel (if you have it) and a bouquet of herbs (parsley, corriander and tarragon) tied with string so they don't all separate. Cover with water.
• Bring to the boil and turn down the heat and let simmer for an hour. Drain through a sieve and throw out the veg (unless you like them soggy!)

Carrot Soup

Serves 2–3

60g butter
1 onion, finely chopped
500g carrots, peeled and chopped
125g potatoes, peeled and diced
1 litre water with or without stock cube, or home-made stock
125ml milk
salt and pepper

• Melt the butter in a pan and soften the onion in the butter for a few minutes.
• Add the carrots, potatoes and seasoning. Stir and mix well together. Then pour in the water or stock, simmer with the lid on until the veggies are well cooked – about 30 minutes.
• Allow to cool, blend in a food processor or blender, then add the milk and reheat. Add more water if required.

Cream of Chicken Soup
Serves 1–2

45g butter

200g dwarf leeks, washed and sliced (ordinary slender leeks, very finely sliced, are good – discard most of the green part)

300ml chicken stock

300ml full-fat milk

2 bay leaves (not essential)

1 clove garlic, peeled

1 free-range chicken breast fillet

1 tablespoon plain flour

pinch of salt

3–4 tablespoons cream (optional)

1 egg yolk (optional)

pinch of ground mace (optional)

• Put 30g of the butter in a heavy-bottomed saucepan, melt it and cook the leeks in it gently until soft. Meanwhile, put the stock and milk in a saucepan with the bay leaves, garlic clove and chicken breast. Bring to the boil, then turn down the heat, and let simmer for about five minutes until the chicken breast is tender.

• A couple of minutes before the chicken is ready, the leeks should be cooked. Add the flour and cook over a low heat, stirring, for 2 minutes.

• Remove the chicken from its pan. Pour the stock and milk mixture into the leek pan, stirring at the same time to mix it together. Bring to just below the boil and, when not stirring, chop or finely shred the chicken and add it to the leeks with a pinch of salt. Keep cooking over a low heat, stirring occasionally, for about 15 minutes.

• Finally, add the remaining 15g butter and cook for another 5 minutes. If the soup is too thick add a bit more milk. Blend the soup in a food processor or blender, then put it back in the pan and reheat until warm enough to eat (or eat it cold if you have run out of gas and the microwave doesn't work!).

• If you want to add cream and the egg yolk, then mix them together and stir into the soup off the heat. Add a little mace, if you like.

Vegetable Soup
Serves 2–3

1 onion

2 carrots

1 turnip

1 parsnip

1 potato

1 leek (white part only)

1 stick celery

drop of olive oil

2 x 2cm knob of butter (not doorknob size)

1 litre home-made chicken or vegetable stock (see page 13), or the easy stock cube option

bouquet of fresh herbs (optional)

pinch of freshly grated nutmeg

salt and pepper

handful of fresh parsley, to serve

• Peel and roughly chop the onion, carrots, turnip, parsnip, potato and leek (or whatever vegetables take your fancy). Roughly chop the celery. Put them all in a food processor and blitz briefly until chopped medium fine. **If a processor is non-existent in your well-equipped student kitchen then just cook the chopped veg and mash when soft**. You don't need the machine either if you finely chop everything instead.

• Heat the oil and butter in a pan. When hot add the vegetables and turn with a spoon to coat them in the oil. Sprinkle with a little salt, cover the pan and leave over a low heat to half-fry/braise until softened. About 10–15 minutes should do the trick.

• From time to time, shake the pan with the lid on, and occasionally uncover and stir. **Make sure nothing is sticking or burning**.

• Pour in the stock, add herbs tied in a bouquet if feeling adventurous and a good grinding of pepper. With the lid off this time simmer and cook for 30–40 minutes. When the veg are cooked, blend the soup in a food processor or blender, grate in a bit of nutmeg and serve, sprinkled with parsley.

• If you don't blend the vegetables and prefer to keep them in chunks you could add meat for a stew effect or try adding pasta with grated Parmesan cheese on top. Boil the pasta or cook the meat first before you add to the soup.

Leek and Potato Soup

Serves 2–3

A favourite that tastes good and is easy to make.

375g leeks
30g butter
1 onion, finely chopped
375g potatoes, peeled and diced
570ml stock
good splash of milk
2 teaspoons sugar (optional)

• Trim off the tops and the roots of the leeks and peel away their tough outer layer. Cut the leeks in half lengthways and **rinse well** in a colander under cold water, as leeks are usually muddy. Then chop into rings.
• Gently melt the butter in a heavy-bottomed pan. Add the leeks and onion, and stir them until soft – 5 minutes max. Add the potatoes after a couple of minutes and sauté them. When they are coated in butter, add the stock, milk and sugar (if using) and let the soup simmer for 20 minutes, or until cooked.
• Blend the soup in a food processor or blender *after* it has cooled a little – I tried doing it when very hot and it explodes out of the blender! Reheat on the stove until hot enough to eat. If it's too thick add more milk.

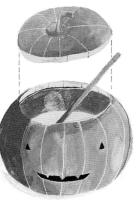

Pumpkin Soup

Serves 6

Beware, this is a weird cooking method!

1 pumpkin (ideally 20cm in diameter and 20cm high)
2 tablespoons soft butter
1 medium onion, finely sliced
50g long grain rice (optional)
900ml chicken stock
a little freshly grated nutmeg (optional)
salt and pepper
fried bacon, grated cheese or cream, to serve (optional)

• Cut a lid from the stalk end of the pumpkin (not too big). Remove the seeds and fibres with your hands. **Yep, cooking is about getting mucky**.
• Rub the inside walls with butter, then sprinkle with salt and pepper. Put the sliced onion in the pumpkin with the uncooked rice.
• Put the pumpkin in a baking tin or ovenproof dish. Bring the stock to boiling point and pour into the pumpkin. Replace the lid.
• Bake for 2 hours (**while you get on with work - not!**) at 190°C/375°F/Gas 5.
• Remove the pumpkin from the oven and with a spoon scrape some of the pumpkin flesh from the walls into the soup. Taste and correct the seasoning. Add a little nutmeg if you like, and you can scatter some fried bacon or grated cheese or 1 or 2 tablespoons cream over the top. Replace the lid and bring to the table.
• When you serve it, scrape some more of the pumpkin from the sides so everyone has some.

Lentil, Tomato and Pasta Soup

Serves 6

If you are a veggie, omit the bacon and use vegetable stock obviously!

3 tablespoons olive oil

2 onions, finely chopped

6 cloves garlic, crushed (this is quite drastic so put in what you want)

2 sticks celery, finely chopped

115g smoked streaky bacon, chopped small (if it hasn't been eaten for breakfast/hangover cure)

225g Puy lentils

4 tomatoes, skinned, seeded and chopped (see page 9)

425g tin Italian plum tomatoes

1.8 litres chicken or vegetable stock

3–4 sprigs of fresh thyme

2 bay leaves

225g macaroni or similar pasta

2–3 tablespoons chopped fresh parsley (you'll have to chop it yourself, as supermarkets are lazy, too!)

90–115g Parmesan cheese, grated

salt and pepper

• Heat the oil in a large heavy-bottomed pan, add the onions, garlic, celery and bacon, and cook over a low heat, until the vegetables are soft and translucent – about 10–15 minutes.

• Add the lentils and stir to coat them in the oil. Add the fresh and tinned tomatoes, chopping the canned ones in their juice. (I'm lazy and usually stick a knife in the pan and swipe it about till they don't look too chunky!) Cook at a gentle bubble for a couple of minutes, adding the stock, thyme and bay leaves.

• Bring to the boil, then cover and simmer until the lentils are cooked – about 40 minutes should do the trick. If the mixture is absorbing a lot of liquid then ladle in some more hot stock or add water if you don't have any stock left. **Keep the level of liquid just above the lentils**.

• Meanwhile, cook the pasta in a pan of boiling water, drain and add to the soup with an extra couple of ladles of stock. Season well, and serve in bowls sprinkled with parsley and Parmesan.

Cheese and Herb Dip

150ml single cream
350g cream cheese
squeeze of lemon juice **(not Jiff lemon – it's rank!)**
2 spring onions, finely chopped
2 tablespoons chopped fresh parsley
2 tablespoons snipped fresh chives
1 clove garlic, crushed
salt and pepper

• Mix the cream and cheese into the lemon juice with a fork or whisk, then mix in the onions, herbs and garlic. Add more lemon juice if needed and seasoning.
• Serve with carrot sticks, cucumber and celery.

Garlic Bread

250g butter
2 cloves garlic, crushed
bunch of fresh parsley, stalks removed and leaves finely chopped
1–2 French stick(s)

• Mash the butter, garlic and parsley together in a bowl. Slash the bread, not all the way through but over halfway, leaving 2–3cm between each slash. Spread the garlic butter on both sides of where you have cut.
• Wrap in foil and bake in a preheated oven, 180°C/350°F/Gas 4, for 10–15 minutes.

Hummus

180g chickpeas, soaked in a bowl full of water overnight (the water must just cover them)
juice of 2 lemons
2–3 cloves garlic, crushed
4 tablespoons tahini (sesame seed paste – you can find this in most supermarkets, healthfood shops and delicatessens)
salt and pepper

• Drain the soaked chickpeas and boil in fresh water for about 1 hour, or until soft. Drain, reserving the cooking water.
• Blend the chickpeas to a purée in a food processor. Add the remaining ingredients and 1–2 tablespoons of the chickpea cooking water, and blend to a soft creamy paste.
• Taste and adjust the seasoning if necessary, adding a touch more lemon juice or some freshly ground pepper.
• Serve with Arab bread or pitta bead – both are nice warmed.

Hummus sounds like a sweat to make, but in the long run it isn't. You can make a huge batch and leave it in the fridge. It's yummy as a substitute for mayonnaise in a sandwich.

Nibbly Bits are good. You can eat them with toast, pitta bread, chopped veggies or tortilla chips or something different of your choice, which is always a bonus. Make it, don't buy it from Sainsbury's!

Aubergine Dip

2 large aubergines
2 tablespoons olive oil
1 clove garlic, crushed
2 tablespoons chopped fresh parsley
1 tablespoon tahini
juice of ½ lemon
salt

• Grill the aubergines. To do this you need to prick each aubergine with a knife around its body otherwise it will explode. Grill them whole for 20 minutes until the skin is black and blistered and they feel soft inside when pressed with a finger. You can also roast them at the hottest temperature you can get your budget student oven to, for 30 minutes.
• Take them out and let them cool before you peel them, as they retain heat for a long time and will viciously burn your fingers.
• Find a colander (the steel bowl with holes) and put it in the sink (this will get messy otherwise). Chop and mash the peeled aubergines into a purée in the colander, using a potato masher or wooden spoon. The juice should leak out of the holes into the sink.
• Transfer the mash into a bowl without holes and beat in the oil, lemon juice, garlic, tahini, parsley and salt.

Cooking for Friends

This is a text book dinner party – tried and tested! What I find most interesting about cooking for a group of people is watching their facial expressions and listening to their comments. The conversation is undoubtedly enhanced by a large supply of good home-made food and alcohol, and spirits are always high.

I arrived back from London the other day at five o'clock in the afternoon. Exhausted from partying and shopping, I began to cook for a dinner party I had arranged.

I was also nervous, as I was hoping that this would be the dinner party to start many more between my group of friends who are all over the country at different universities. I hadn't seen some of them for a year and half of them hadn't got their invitations due to the Christmas post, so I was relying on word of mouth and mobiles. None of them had replied – you know how disorganized students are on the social front! There may be something better going on etc… So I didn't really know how many were coming and if any of them had turned veggie at uni.

I had asked Helen and Al to arrive early, as I knew I could rely on them to be great sous-chefs. They arrived just as the choccie pudding was about to be taken out of the oven, timed so we could rush off to the supermarket 15 minutes away to get some last-minute supplies, such as the main course!

I chopped, Helen peeled and I faffed as I hadn't cooked for ages, and we started drinking. Before we knew it, it was 7.30pm. Panic stations! I still had to organise the casserole of pork chops and apples, the little roast potatoes and the other half of the pudding and, rather unusually, everyone was punctual.

An hour and a demolished bowl of hummus and tortilla chips later, the dinner was miraculously ready and we tucked into a nice little feast. So there you go. A mad last-minute supper party can be done with a couple of amazing helpers, a great mum who washes up and some guests to enjoy it. Finishing touches like candles and place mats made the table look pretty cool. My wicked mates brought the booze and we all had a good time

Pork Chops with Apple

Serves 4

500g onions, sliced

500g cooking apples, peeled and sliced (if you don't have cooking apples use normal ones and omit the sugar)

1 tablespoon sugar

4 pork chops

1 tablespoon wholegrain mustard

knobs of butter

salt and pepper

• Spread the sliced onions in an ovenproof casserole dish. Add salt and pepper, then cover them with half the sliced apples and sprinkle with the sugar.

• Add the pork chops, and coat with the mustard. Season with salt and pepper then add the rest of the apple and a few ice cube size knobs of butter.

• Put the lid on the casserole dish, or foil if it has no lid, and bake the pork for 1–1½ hours at 200°C/400°F/Gas 6 until tender.

Roasted Rosemary Potatoes

Serves 4

I chopped a huge bag of organic potatoes for us – pretty boring but worthwhile when you taste them and want more and more!

2 tablespoons olive oil

4/5 large organic potatoes (good roasting ones), left unpeeled and chopped into 1cm squares

2 cloves garlic, left unpeeled

2 sprigs of fresh rosemary

salt and pepper

• Warm the olive oil on a baking sheet in a preheated oven, 200°C/400°F/Gas 6, for a few minutes.

• Add the chopped potatoes, unpeeled garlic cloves and rosemary. Cook for about 60 minutes, turning them in the oil every now and then. Season them right at the end of cooking.

I put the potatoes in the oven at the same time as the pork and turned them every 10–15 minutes. Then half an hour before the end of cooking I boiled a bag of carrots, chopped and peeled, with sugar and butter for 5–7 minutes before I took them off the hob, I added a bit more water and some frozen peas. When they were cooked I drained them and put a knob of butter on top.

Chocolate Pudding

Serves 4–6

**This pudding I cooked first and then left. You
can do this whenever you like during the day.
This is a rich chocolate pudding, made especially
for my friend Jess, but girlies in general love it!**

150g plain chocolate, broken into pieces
150g margarine or preferably butter
1 teaspoon vanilla, brandy or rum essence
150ml warm water
110g caster sugar
4 eggs, separated
25g self-raising flour
½ teaspoon cream of tartar

• Melt the chocolate with the margarine or butter
and the essence in a bowl set over a pan of very
hot water or in the top of a double saucepan.
• When melted, add the warm water, then the
caster sugar and stir until smooth.
• Pour the chocolate mixture into a mixing bowl.
Stir in the egg yolks.
• Stir in the self-raising flour and beat or whisk
until the mixture is free of lumps.
• Add the cream of tartar to the egg whites and
whisk in a clean bowl until they stand in peaks.
• Fold the egg whites lightly into the chocolate
mixture with a metal spoon, then pour into a
greased, medium-sized, ovenproof pudding basin.
• Boil a kettle and half-fill a roasting tin with
boiling water. Put this in a preheated oven,
200°C/400°F/Gas 6, for a couple of minutes
to heat the tin.
• Stand the pudding in the roasting tin so it is
surrounded by water. You do not want to get
water in the pudding, so do not fill the roasting
tin too full. Cook for 10 minutes, then reduce the
oven temperature to 160°C/325°F/Gas 3 and
cook for 30 minutes longer. Test the middle with
a skewer – the skewer must be mainly clean
when removed for the pudding to be cooked.
• Serve hot or cold. I usually whip double cream
and put a thin layer on top, then grate some
chocolate over to make it look funky.

Poached Pears

Serves 6

These need hardly any responsibility and taste great with a rich pudding like the chocolate one. They are also really good served on their own with a bit of crème fraîche.

6 firm but ripe pears – you don't want them to fall apart

lemon juice, to stop the pears discolouring

600ml water

100g vanilla caster sugar

2 slices each of large curly bits of orange and lemon peel

1 vanilla pod, cut lengthways with its innards scooped out

1 tablespoon orange flower water (optional)

• Peel the pears, leaving the stalks in place, then sprinkle with lemon juice so that they don't go brown.

• Make the sugar syrup by boiling the water and sugar furiously with the peels, vanilla pod and its insides. Boil until you have a thick syrup, but don't let it go brown.

• Add the orange flower water, if using, and the pears. Cook in a heavy-bottomed casserole dish at a gentle simmer until pears are just tender when pierced with a skewer.

• Leave to cool, before serving.

Pasta

Well, I don't think I, or any of my friends, could live without pasta. You really can't have a huge disaster with it either, and it is a reliable staple as it doesn't go off at the back of the cupboard. You can cook a truck-load of it and keep some aside to make a cold pasta salad for the next week. I recommend trying it with some peas, Hellmann's mayonnaise and tuna.

Pasta is really the best basic thing you could start to learn to cook with, and can help encourage your creativity. All you need is: enough money to buy the pasta, some taste buds that work, some imagination, some guinea pigs and enough energy to trudge down to the supermarket and find some yummy ingredients to make a sauce with.

Spaghetti Carbonara

Serves 2–3

Every student thinks they know how to make a carbonara and they probably can, but here is an alternative one with a bit more going for it than just bacon, cream and cheese. It is rich, but it's easy to cook and you can omit the cream if you want.

200g spaghetti

4–5 rashers bacon or pancetta (ask at a delicatessen)

2 teaspoons olive oil

4 tablespoons white wine (it's an excuse to buy a bottle and you can drink most of it!)

1 whole egg

1 egg yolk (see below)

4 tablespoons freshly grated Parmesan cheese (use cheddar, if you prefer)

250ml single cream (optional)

1 rounded tablespoon butter

black pepper

• Cook the pasta in a pan of boiling water. Meanwhile, cut off the bacon rind and cut the bacon or pancetta into chunky pieces. Fry in the olive oil for 5 minutes until crispy.

• Throw in the wine and bubble for 3 minutes. Remove from the heat and set aside.

• In a bowl, beat together the whole egg, egg yolk, cheese, cream (if you're using it) and pepper with a fork.

• When the pasta is ready, return the pan with the bacon and wine to a medium heat and add the butter.

• Drain the pasta and return it to its hot pan. Add the bacon and wine to the pasta, then pour in the egg mixture and quickly and thoroughly turn the pasta so it is entirely covered by the sauce. **Don't put the pan on the heat**, be patient and the eggs will set from the heat of the pasta. If the pan is too hot they will scramble.

Tip: When separating eggs, **be careful**. Hit the egg on the side of a bowl, break it using both thumbs and transfer the yolk to and from each shell half until the egg white has slipped into the bowl beneath, leaving the yolk in one half of the shell. Tip the yolk into another bowl until needed. Separating eggs is frustrating at first but practise and it's quite a fun skill to acquire.

The Best Bolognese

Serves 6

Takes a while to cook but it's well worth it, and you can make loads of stuff with it, too.

3–4 tablespoons olive oil (you might need to add more if the pan gets dry, but the meat should have some fat in it)

7g butter

2–3 onions, chopped

2 sticks celery, finely chopped

2 carrots, peeled and finely chopped

600g minced beef or lamb

100ml full-fat milk

freshly grated nutmeg

250ml dry white wine

2 x 425g tins whole Italian plum tomatoes

10 tomatoes, skinned, seeded and chopped

salt and pepper

- **The mince should not be from too lean a cut.**
- **Use a pot that retains heat.**
- **Cook, uncovered, at the merest simmer for a long, long time – no less than 3 hours.**
- **You can use bolognese for lasagne, shepherd's pie, baked potatoes etc…**

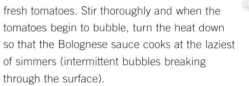

• Heat the oil and butter in a pan. Add the chopped onions and turn the heat to medium. Sauté the onion until translucent. Add the finely chopped celery and carrots and cook for 2 minutes, stirring to coat them well in the oil.

• Add the minced meat, a large pinch of salt and good grinding of pepper. Crumble the mince with a fork, stir well and cook until it has lost its raw red colour.

• Add the milk and let it simmer until it has evaporated, making sure you stir it frequently. Add a tiny grating of nutmeg.

• When the milk has boiled off, add the wine and let this, too, simmer until it has evaporated, then add the tinned tomatoes, chopping them up inside the pan. Add the skinned and chopped fresh tomatoes. Stir thoroughly and when the tomatoes begin to bubble, turn the heat down so that the Bolognese sauce cooks at the laziest of simmers (intermittent bubbles breaking through the surface).

• Cook, uncovered, for about 3 hours, stirring from time to time. While the sauce is cooking it may begin to dry out as the fat separates from the meat. Add 60ml water whenever necessary. At the end **no water must be left.** Add salt to taste. The Bolognese can be refrigerated for up to three days.

Tip: Chop all the vegetables before doing anything. It makes life easier and you won't burn the onions while chopping everything else.

Béchamel Sauce

Makes 300ml

1 tablespoon butter
1½ tablespoons plain flour
300ml full-fat milk
freshly grated nutmeg
salt and pepper

• Melt the butter over a low heat in a heavy-bottomed pan, non-stick if possible. Add the flour, stirring all the time so it doesn't stick for 2–3 minutes, until you have a golden paste.
• Slowly add the milk, keeping the paste quite thick and stirring with a whisk to keep out the lumps. Keep stirring and whisking and adding milk over the lowest heat possible.
• When all the milk has been smoothly incorporated, add salt and pepper and grate in some nutmeg. Return to the heat until the sauce has thickened. If it gets too thick too quickly, add a dash more milk and whisk the lumps out.

Warning: If you haven't made enough sauce, **do not under any circumstances try and add more flour and milk** as it tastes disgusting. Heat more butter in another pan then add flour, then slowly add the sauce you have, with more milk, to the butter and flour mixture and whisk.

Variations
• To make cheese sauce just stir grated Cheddar into the béchamel sauce at the end when the pan is off the heat, **otherwise it will curdle.** You could add a bit of cayenne for flavour, but go easy on it.
• To make parsley sauce add finely chopped parsley to a béchamel sauce. It goes really well with ham and baked potatoes.

Lasagne
Serves 4–5

butter, for greasing
600g precooked lasagne sheets
1 quantity bolognese sauce (see page 26), or make
a quickie where you throw everything in together,
missing out the milk and wine, just using the juice
of the tinned tomatoes and a bit of water
150–200g Parmesan cheese, grated

For the béchamel sauce:
85g butter
75g plain flour
¼ teaspoon salt
milk to mix

• Use a Pyrex or at least an ovenproof dish – a
square/rectangular dish is easiest as the lasagne
sheets will fit without having to break them up.
• Make a béchamel sauce using the quantities
above, following the method given opposite.
• Line the bottom of the dish with a thin layer of
béchamel and swoosh it around till it covers the
bottom of the dish. Cover the sauce with the
strips of pasta. Cut or break them if need be to
fit, with no more than 6mm overlapping – **no
overlapping if possible.**
• Add a thin layer of the Bolognese sauce, then
a layer of béchamel, but not too much, then a
layer of pasta. Do this meat sauce–béchamel–
pasta thing for at least three to five layers. I do
less if my dish is not very deep.
• Leave enough béchamel for the top, which is a
thicker layer than the others. Most recipes tell
you not to put meat sauce on the top layer; I do,
but do whatever you feel like. If you don't have
any meat sauce left, pour over a thick layer of
béchamel, then cover with grated Parmesan,
which will melt into a gooey, yummy topping.
• Cook in a preheated oven, 200°C /400°F/Gas 6,
for 10–15 minutes. Spike with a knife or skewer –
it should go through easily. If not, cook for
another 5–10 minutes – no longer. The cheese on
top should be golden, and the juices bubbling.

Tip: The sheets of precooked lasagne are a lot
less hassle. Otherwise, you have to cook the
pasta first before assembling the lasagne.

Prawn and Leek Lasagne

Serves 4

60g butter or 4 tablespoons olive oil.

12 thick leeks (white parts only), washed and chopped into 1cm chunks

150–200g Parmesan cheese, grated

600g precooked lasagne sheets

900g cooked, peeled prawns (I use defrosted frozen ones from the supermarket)

For the béchamel sauce:

900ml milk

1 bay leaf (optional)

1 onion, halved

pinch of freshly grated nutmeg

60g butter

50g plain flour (may need more or less, **add slowly**)

salt and pepper

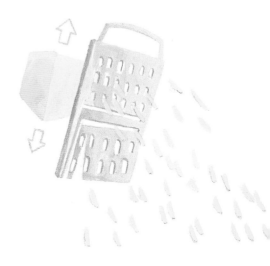

• Put the milk for the béchamel sauce in a pan with the bay leaf, onion and grated nutmeg. Bring to just below boiling point – you will see this when a slight skin forms on the milk. Take the pan off the heat and leave the milk to infuse for 10 minutes. You do this as the leeks and prawns have little flavour.

• In another pan melt the butter for the sauce. Stir in the flour for 1 minute or less to form a paste. Then gradually stir in the infused milk to make a thick smooth béchamel sauce. You may have to whisk the lumps out.

• Heat the butter or oil. Add the leeks and cook over a low heat until softened and translucent.

• Put a thin layer of béchamel sauce in a large greased baking or Pyrex dish and sprinkle over about one-third of the grated Parmesan. Add a layer of lasagne and scatter over some of the prawns and leeks. Pour over a thin layer of sauce and a sprinkle of Parmesan before adding another layer of pasta.

• Repeat for four or five layers ending with a layer of pasta, then béchamel and the Parmesan. Cook in a preheated oven, 190°C/375°F/Gas 5, for 30–40 minutes. Test by sticking a knife in the middle. The lasagne should be soft, the juices bubbling and the cheese golden.

Penne Pasta with Roasted Vegetables

Serves 4

1 fennel bulb (if you are feeling fancy)

4 onions, peeled and quartered (red ones are nice for this)

4 large leeks, washed and chopped into 4cm chunks

2 courgettes, cut into chunks

2 x 200g packs cherry tomatoes

olive oil, for drizzling

pinch of dried herbs such as thyme and oregano

325g penne pasta

1 clove garlic, crushed

a few fresh basil leaves, finely torn

salt and pepper

175g cheese, grated – either Parmesan, mozzarella or Gruyère, or a mixture of them all. Just buy a single block or a bit of each (Cheddar is probably not a good choice)

• Strip the fennel to the inner heart and quarter the heart. Throw away the other leaves or, if you are a biology student, save them for your lab bunnies.

• Put all the vegetables in a roasting tin. Drizzle the olive oil over the top, and roll the vegetables around to make sure they are well coated. Scatter on a few herbs if you have some, and whack in a preheated oven, 190°C/375°F/Gas 5, for 30 minutes.

• Poke the vegetables with a knife – they should be tender and beginning to brown. Keep the leeks oily – drizzle on more oil during cooking if necessary, as they turn brown if they are dry.

• Five to ten minutes before the vegetables are ready, boil the penne pasta until *al dente* – not too floppy – and drain.

• Mix together the roasted vegetables, cooked pasta, garlic and basil and some salt and pepper in a mixing bowl. Stir in the grated cheese.

• Turn the pasta mixture into a greased gratin dish and bake in the oven for 20 minutes. This is yummy just served with a salad.

Pesto

Serves 4

You need a food processor to make this once-a-year recipe. You can keep it in the fridge but please not for a year! It gets a bit boring if you eat it a lot!

110g fresh basil leaves
8 tablespoons extra virgin olive oil
3 tablespoons pine nuts
2 cloves garlic, finely chopped
60g Parmesan cheese, grated
2 tablespoons Romano cheese, grated
45g softened butter
salt and pepper

• Wash the basil in cold water, then pat it dry with kitchen paper.
• Put the basil, olive oil, pine nuts and garlic in a food processor with a pinch of salt. Blend together until you have a creamy consistency.
• Transfer into a bowl and add the grated Parmesan and Romano cheese. When all the cheese is mixed in, stir in the softened butter. Season to taste.
• To serve, toss the pesto with cooked pasta, or spread some on a grilled chicken sandwich or on large, grilled mushrooms.

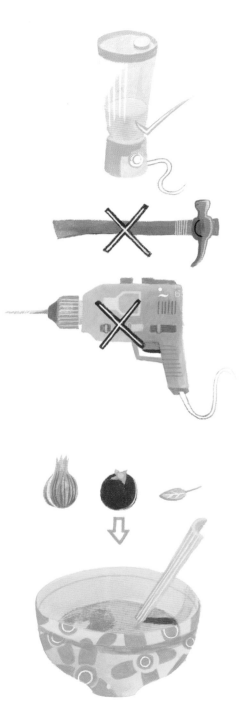

Raw Tomato Sauce

Serves 4

6–8 ripe tomatoes

6–10 fresh basil leaves, torn into pieces (you can't use a steel knife as the basil will go brown, use your fingers and rip them into small pieces)

olive oil, to mix

1 onion, finely chopped (optional)

handful of parsley

salt and pepper

• To make this sauce you first need to blanch the tomatoes. To do this, add boiling water to a bowl. Add the tomatoes, pricked with a knife. (I recently learnt an easier way from a good friend, Sarah, who crosses the bottoms, so the skin peels off in quarters rather than randomly.)
• Take them out after 30 seconds so they don't go soggy, or just keep a running tap of cold water on them so they stop cooking and you can handle them. Remove the skins, cut the tomatoes into quarters and seed them using your fingers. Then chop the flesh into cubes. The hardest stuff is over, but it looks impressive while you are doing it!
• All you need to do now is put the cubes in a deep bowl, season to your taste and add torn basil leaves and parsley. Turn the mixture by hand, cover with a good amount of olive oil and leave.
• Serve with pasta or grilled fish. If you really want to impress you can also add a finely chopped raw onion.

Cooked Tomato Sauce

Serves 4

dash of olive oil

1 onion, finely chopped

2 sticks celery, chopped (the celery is optional, but does add more flavour)

900g tomatoes, skinned, seeded and chopped (see Raw Tomato Sauce for instructions)

500g tinned whole tomatoes, chopped in their juice

75g butter

pesto or torn fresh basil leaves, to taste (optional)

salt

• Heat the olive oil in a heavy-bottomed saucepan or frying pan.
• Add the onion when the oil is hot. Sauté until translucent, add the celery and blanched tomatoes. Also add the chopped tinned ones and their juice. Add the butter and a little salt and simmer over a very low heat for about 45 minutes until the sauce has thickened. You only need to stir the sauce once in a while.
• You can add some pesto right at the end for extra flavour, or just some freshly torn basil.

Noodles and Stir-Fries

Noodles are wicked. Yes, they come in pots and smell like dog food, but they also come in packets – no, not 'Supernoodles', normal plain Chinese ones. Don't get me wrong, I have eaten the potted and cheap flavoured packet types at many a drunken, desperate moment, but the proper Chinese ones are much better.

You can do loads with them, like adding them to stock with some stir-fried vegetables fried in peanut oil and soy sauce. They do taste nicer than 'pot noodles', and the portions are larger than a king-size pot noodle, too. Noodles make a **quick meal before going out clubbing** and are cheap if your budget is low and you want to save your money for beer!

Noodle Soup with Grilled Fish

Serves 2

Slightly more extravagant than 'pot noodles' is this recipe, which I am dedicating to my Duke of Edinburgh group who were my 'Supernoodle' partners for five years of camping on Dartmoor.

3 tablespoons dark soy sauce

1 clove garlic, crushed

1 teaspoon sugar

2 tablespoons sake or rice wine (optional)

2 tablespoons dry sherry (optional)

200g any white fish, skinned e.g. cod, haddock or plaice

150g thin noodles

300ml chicken stock (see page 13)

a little olive oil

1–2 spring onions, finely chopped

lump of fresh root ginger, peeled and crushed

large handful of spinach leaves (remove any thick stems)

• Mix the soy sauce, garlic and sugar in a shallow dish together with the sake and sherry if you are using them. Put the fish into the mixture, turning to coat both sides, and leave for 30 minutes.

• Boil a large saucepan of water for the noodles. Salt the water as it reaches the boil and add the noodles. Cook them for 4 minutes. Drain, then put into cold water.

• Put the stock on to boil.

• Put a little oil in a frying pan and fry the spring onions and ginger until soft. Add the spinach leaves, torn if they are a bit large, and cook for 1 minute till they wilt.

• Push the spinach to the side of the pan and add the marinated fish. Cook for 1–2 minutes on each side.

• When the stock has boiled, ladle it into two bowls. Stir in the spring onion, ginger and spinach mixture, and the noodles. Lay the fish on top. **Eat**.

Vegetable Stir-Fry

Serves 2

Use any vegetables you want. You can buy some funky packs with beansprouts and other weird Chinese vegetables in a supermarket.

4 tablespoons oil

3 tablespoons butter

1 onion or 2 baby shallots, chopped

2 cloves garlic, finely chopped

½ tablespoon finely chopped, or better still crushed, fresh root ginger

handful each of mangetout, beansprouts, peeled and chopped carrots, chopped peppers, broccoli and cauliflower florets

¼ chicken or vegetable stock cube, crumbled

1 tablespoon soy sauce

1 heaped teaspoon of sugar (muscovado sugar is best, but caster is fine if it's all you've got)

1 heaped teaspoon cornflour

1 teaspoon Chinese spices

salt and pepper

• Heat the oil and butter in a large frying pan or wok if you have one. Add the onion, garlic and ginger and fry until translucent (5 minutes max).

• Add the carrots, broccoli, cauliflower or whatever else you have bought that needs to be cooked slightly to a large pan of boiling water. Boil for 5–7 minutes. Don't let them go soggy, the whole point of a stir-fry is that the veggies are a bit crunchy. Drain then rinse under cold water.

• Add the mangetout, beansprouts and peppers (these don't need to be precooked) and the half-cooked carrots, broccoli etc. to the onions.

• Add the stock cube, soy sauce, sugar, cornflour, spices and salt and pepper or your bought cheating sauce (see Tip below), and simmer gently until everything is cooked to your liking **(no more than 15 minutes)**.

• Serve with a meat dish or rice/Chinese noodles if you are a veggie. Couscous is nice with this as well.

Tip: Instead of the last six ingredients you could use a shop-bought stir-fry sauce – much to my mum's disgust, but they are useful if you're feeling lazy!

Chicken Stir-Fry

Serves 2

2 tablespoons olive oil

1 tablespoon sesame oil (or just use a bit more olive oil)

1cm x 1cm cube of fresh root ginger, sliced

1 clove garlic, sliced

1 spring onion, chopped

2 chicken breast fillets, chopped (or use cooked leftovers from a roast, and just add them at the end to warm through)

mixed vegetables (I suggest a handful each of beansprouts, carrots, courgettes, peppers, mushrooms – anything you have lying around)

soy sauce, to taste

Chinese/rice noodles or rice (see packet for size of serving)

• Heat both oils in a wok or frying pan. When fairly hot, add the ginger, garlic and onion, and fry for just a few minutes. Remove the garlic and ginger – they are used just to flavour the oil.

• Keep the oil, and add the raw chicken. Cook for 5 minutes. Then add the vegetables and fry for another 10–20 minutes. The veg will get dry while frying, so add a little water and some soy sauce. (Or you could add a black bean sauce, which you can get from the supermarket or a little more oil, or a drop of Worcestershire sauce.)

• Meanwhile, boil a saucepan of water and cook the noodles or rice, according to packet instructions. Serve them separately or stir-fry with the veggies at the last minute. I usually put rice or noodles on the plate, make a hole and put the veg and chicken in the middle – it looks pretty!

Rice

You will probably be cooking a lot of rice, so here are a few small points, which will help you cook it to perfection.

Remember to read the instructions on the packet carefully. Always cook a slightly larger quantity than suggested, as it can be reheated and eaten the next day. Wash rice in a sieve before you cook it as the starch in the rice can make it gloopy and sticky. Rice often dries out while cooking, so keep checking it to see if it needs a bit more water – you can always drain it off at the end. Also remember to add a bit of oil to the water, as you do with pasta, so it doesn't stick, and to add some salt for flavour. It's always a good idea to rinse rice at the end when it's cooked – put the rice in a sieve and pour boiling water over it. Approximately 500g of rice serves 5–6 people. You can add virtually anything you like to rice really, so just go mad and experiment.

Basic Risotto (from leftovers)

Serves 3–4

1–2 onions (depending on size)

dash of olive oil (to cover the bottom of the pan)

2 carrots, peeled and chopped (add more veg like peas or sweetcorn from the freezer or a tin or, if you are feeling really adventurous, use fresh)

300g rice (as a general rule I use half a cup of rice per person)

750ml hot chicken stock (see page 13)

3 cooked chicken breasts, shredded (see Tip)

chopped fresh parsley, to taste

handful of grated Parmesan cheese, to taste

salt and pepper

soy sauce/chilli sauce, to serve (optional)

• In a large pan sauté the onion in hot olive oil. Add the carrot and any other fresh veg you are using for your risotto.

• Wash the rice in a sieve under cold water to remove the starch.

• Add the rice to the pan and stir with a wooden spoon, making sure all the ingredients are coated with the oil. After 4–5 minutes of stirring, add enough stock to just cover the rice, and season with salt and pepper. Simmer over a medium heat for 5 minutes.

• Keep stirring the rice and adding more of the stock. If the stock boils off too quickly you need to add more liquid – you could boil a kettle and use a stock cube (see box of cubes for instructions), or just use boiling water. It means that the risotto is boiling too furiously **so turn the heat down.**

• While the rice is cooking, in another pan boil the frozen peas and sweetcorn for 3–4 minutes.

• When the rice is cooked (it should be swollen and soft) add the cooked chicken and peas or sweetcorn and warm through over a low heat. Add some parsley and grated Parmesan to taste, and serve.

• I put soy sauce on the table as the risotto tastes good with a few drops on top. Or try chilli sauce (Tabasco) to give it a real kick!

Tip: To save time and money use leftover chicken – simply pick the meat off the bones after a roast. Alternatively, cook three chicken breasts in a preheated oven at 180°C/350°F/ Gas 4 in a dish with some olive oil, with tin foil over the top to steam the breasts in their own juices, for 15–20 minutes.

Easy Mushroom Risotto

Serves 4

Mushrooms and my brother have a hate–hate relationship, so when my mum suggested that I cooked mushroom risotto for one of my cooking competitions I said yes, just to piss him off! (Sorry, Harry, can't remember why you were annoying me that day!)

dash of olive oil

25g butter

2 onions, finely chopped

1 clove garlic, finely chopped

115g dried porcini (or ceps as they are otherwise known – see Tip) or Chestnut mushrooms

325g arborio risotto rice

900ml chicken or vegetable stock (see page 13 – some of this can be made up from the rehydrated mushroom water, see Tip)

2 handfuls of frozen peas (optional)

salt and pepper

handful of grated Parmesan cheese, to serve

• Heat the olive oil and butter in a pan and sauté the onions and garlic. After 2 minutes add the mushrooms and stir well to coat them in oil.

• Add the rice and also stir to coat the grains with oil. Pour in the mushroom water, and cook for 5–6 minutes, stirring until the liquid is nearly absorbed.

• Add the peas, if using, and the stock, a cup at a time, until absorbed – you don't want it too watery. Keep watching and stirring all the way through cooking, so the risotto doesn't stick and burn.

• Season with salt and pepper. Ladle into four bowls and sprinkle with Parmesan cheese.

Tip: If you buy the dried porcini you need to rehydrate them. Soak the mushrooms in enough warm water to cover them. When they are rehydrated (which will take about 20–30 minutes) strain the water into another bowl, and use it with the stock to cook the rice. You need to strain the water as it could be gritty.

Pea and Prawn Risotto
Serves 6

25g butter
dash of olive oil
1 onion, finely chopped
1 clove garlic, finely chopped
1 stick celery, finely chopped
450g arborio risotto rice
2 wine glasses white wine
900ml vegetable stock (see page 12)
455g raw peeled prawns
3 handfuls of frozen peas
1 handful of fresh basil, chopped
½ handful of fresh mint, chopped
salt and pepper
squeeze of lemon juice, to serve

• Melt the butter with the oil. Add the onion, garlic and celery, and cook until softened.
• Add the rice and cook for 1 minute.
• Pour over the wine and cook until some of the liquid is reduced.
• Add the vegetable stock, a ladle at a time, and keep stirring the rice until the stock is almost absorbed. Add more stock, and continue stirring for about 15 minutes.
• Then add the prawns, peas and fresh herbs, and cook for a further 5–6 minutes.
• Season with salt and fresh pepper, squeeze over the lemon juice and serve.

Cashew Nut Rice

Serves 4

This is a really easy recipe and takes only 15–20 minutes to cook.

1 small onion, finely chopped
1 clove garlic, finely chopped
2 tablespoons olive oil
1 green pepper, cored, seeded and chopped
225g mushrooms, chopped
625g brown rice, cooked
115g cashew nuts
soy sauce, to taste

• Cook the rice.
• Fry the onion and garlic and in the oil until translucent.
• Add the chopped pepper and mushrooms and cook for 1–2 minutes.
• Add the cooked rice and nuts, and fry until heated through.
• Add soy sauce to taste and serve hot.

Rice Casserole

Serves 6

625g rice
1 onion, chopped
2 cloves garlic, chopped
1 green pepper, cored, seeded and chopped
3 tablespoons olive oil
3 carrots, peeled and diced
225g young green beans, chopped
225g soaked and cooked (or drained, tinned) kidney beans
1 tablespoon chopped fresh parsley
750ml vegetable stock (see page 13)
¼ teaspoon saffron
¼ teaspoon turmeric
¼ teaspoon crushed coriander

• Half-cook the rice in a large pan – check the instructions on the packet and cook for half the time stated. Rinse in cold water and drain. Return to the pan.
• In another pan fry the onion, garlic and pepper gently in the olive oil until soft.
• Add the onion, garlic and pepper, together with the carrots, beans and parsley to the rice and stir well.
• Heat the vegetable stock and add to it the saffron, turmeric and crushed coriander.
• Add the stock slowly to the rice mixture. Bring to the boil, reduce the heat, cover then cook gently until all the liquid is absorbed, about 20 minutes. Serve hot.

Curries Ones that aren't as complicated as Madhur Jaffrey's

Going out with your mates for a few beers and a good curry is the way forward, but if you feel like eating a curry at home while watching the footie, then here are some quickies. Don't get me wrong, Madhur Jaffrey is a legend, but you have to have every Indian spice you could imagine and lots of courage if you are learning to be a curry maestro. And don't be put off by the names of the spices, they are easy to find in delis or supermarkets.

Lamb Curry
Serves 4–5

1 quantity Red Hot Marinade (see page 47)
2 tablespoons butter
2 x 425g tins chopped tomatoes
285ml stock or water
1.5kg leg of lamb, diced
olive oil, for frying
handful of chopped fresh mint and coriander
250ml natural yogurt
lime juice, to taste
salt and pepper

For the curry paste:
5cm cube of fresh root ginger, peeled
2 tennis ball-sized red onions, peeled
10 cloves garlic, peeled
2 fresh red chillies, with their seeds
bunch of fresh coriander

• Roughly chop all the curry paste ingredients, add to the hot marinade and purée in a food processor.
• In a large casserole dish, fry the puréed paste in the butter until it turns golden, stirring regularly. Add the canned tomatoes and the stock or water. Bring to the boil, cover with foil and place in a preheated oven, 160°C/ 325°F/Gas 3, for 1½ hours. To intensify the flavours, remove the foil and continue to simmer over the hob until it
thickens. This is a basic curry sauce.
• Fry the lamb in a little olive oil until golden. Add the curry sauce and simmer for 1 hour or until tender.
• Finally, sprinkle over the chopped mint and coriander and stir in the yogurt. Season to taste and add a good squeeze of lime juice.
• Serve with basmati rice or naan bread.

Tip: Most **curry sauces can be used with anything**, so if you are vegetarian, peas, spinach, cauliflower, potatoes, lentils or fried aubergine are good, or if you need meat, diced chicken or prawns can be tasty.

Marinades

Marinades are a great way to flavour meat. You may think they are just for large steaks and chicken to cook on a barbecue, but I recently discovered you can marinate fish and vegetables, too. Marinades take only a few minutes to prepare and just need to be rubbed into the meat/fish/vegetables. You can marinate things for anything from 30 minutes to 2–3 hours. Obviously the longer you leave it, the stronger the flavour will be. Then all you need do is preheat the oven, light the barbie, grill or whatever you've got, and cook the food.

Yoghurt Marinade

500g tub natural yoghurt (a big one)
2 handfuls of fresh mint, chopped
grated zest and juice of 2 limes
1 tablespoon coriander seeds, crushed
dash of olive oil
salt and pepper

• Put all the ingredients in a bowl and mix well.
• Smear over any type of meat or fish. Leave to marinate for at least 30 minutes before cooking.

Spicy Cajun Marinade

2 tablespoons paprika
2 tablespoons cayenne pepper
1 tablespoon black peppercorns, ground
2 cloves garlic, crushed
3 tablespoons dried onion flakes
2 tablespoons dried oregano
salt

• Pound all the ingredients together until you have a powdery consistency
• Rub all over the meat. Leave to marinate for at least 30 minutes before cooking.

Red Hot Marinade

2 tablespoons fennel seeds
2 tablespoons cumin seeds
½ tablespoon fenugreek seeds
½ tablespoon black peppercorns
½ cinnamon stick
2 cardamom pods
salt and pepper

• Lightly toast the ingredients over a gentle heat in a pan (**no oil needed**). **Watch carefully** as the mixture can suddenly go from toasted to burnt – 5–10 minutes over a low heat is about right.
• Then pound the ingredients using a pestle and mortar into a powder.
• Rub generously over your chosen meat. Leave to marinate for at least 30 minutes before cooking.

Chicken, ginger and yoghurt curry

Serves 8

This recipe is best prepared in advance, to get the most out of the marinade!

1 large chicken (you can use 8 breasts of chicken de-skined, or a meaty leg of lamb)

3 onions peeled and chopped

a finger size chunk of fresh ginger peeled

2 cloves of garlic peeled

2–3 seeded green chillies finely chopped

60g blanched almonds (they come in a bag from the supermarket) finely chopped (you have to do that bit though!)

500ml live natural yoghurt

1 tablespoon ground cumin

1 tablespoon ground coriander seeds

½ teaspoon cayenne pepper

1 teaspoon of the seeds from a cardamom pod (use green pods, break them open and take out the seeds)

1 teaspoon garamasala

1 teaspoon salt

3 tablespoon olive oil

4–5 cloves

1 cinnamon stick

4–5 peppercorns

1 handful each of flaked almonds

sultanas

a bunch of fresh coriander

• Put the chopped onions, garlic, ginger, chillies and almonds and a third of the yoghurt into a food processor and blend to a paste

• Pour the rest of the yoghurt into a bowl and add the paste from the blender. Then add the cumin, coriander, cayenne pepper, cardamom seeds, and garamasala – and whisk lightly to amalgamate.

• Make shallow cuts in the chicken and spread as much paste inside as possible, then pour the rest over the top. Marinate for up to 24 hours in the fridge. Take out an hour before cooking.

• Heat the oil in a frying pan and when hot, cook the cloves, cinnamon and pepper in the oil for a couple of minutes.

• Pour this over the chicken, cover with foil and bake for 30 minutes, 190°C/375°F/Gas 5.

• Remove the foil and sprinkle over the sultanas and flaked almonds. Cook for another 10 minutes without the lid. Skewer the chicken to test that it is cooked properly.

Tip: When you skewer the meat the juices of the chicken will run clear if cooked, and pink if it needs a little longer.

• For a vegetable, chop some cauliflower into small pieces, and boil until they are cooked al dente.

• Heat some olive oil in a frying pan and fry the cauliflower with a teaspoon of cumin seeds and perhaps a little curry powder!

• When ready to eat, sprinkle fresh chopped corriander over the top of the chicken. As this is a fairly complicated dish – in terms of all the spices – serve with the cauliflower, poppadoms and rice.

Fish

My only hatred used to be fish – until I worked in a fishmonger's for three months while bumming at home and earning money to travel. I don't know how it cured my fear, but now I'm converted.

Everyone thinks it's expensive, but if you look at how much you spend on a meal in McD's it's far more than on a simple piece of fish and some salad or potatoes and a vegetable. I promise fish can be cheap if you choose the right cut and the right type.

I haven't provided any shellfish recipes, but mussels are very easy to cook. Just heat some oil and fry some finely chopped onions and garlic. Add the mussels, some white wine and stock or water halfway up the pan – not covering the whole pile of mussels, and cook till the shells start opening. This is very quick. Just **don't eat the ones that stay closed**.

Fish in Breadcrumbs

Serves 2

1 egg

2–3 tablespoons breadcrumbs

1 dessertspoon chopped fresh parsley

grated zest of 1 small lemon

2 fillets of fish (flat fish, such as plaice
or Dover sole)

olive oil, for frying

salt and pepper

• Beat the egg in a shallow dish and add salt
and pepper.

• Mix the breadcrumbs, herbs and lemon rind
together in another shallow dish.

• Pat the fillets of fish dry on kitchen paper. Dip
them in the beaten egg and then in the
breadcrumb mixture, until evenly coated all over.

• Heat the oil in a big frying pan, fry the fillets for
3 minutes on each side until golden brown. Take
out and drain on kitchen paper.

• Serve with vegetables and lemon wedges.

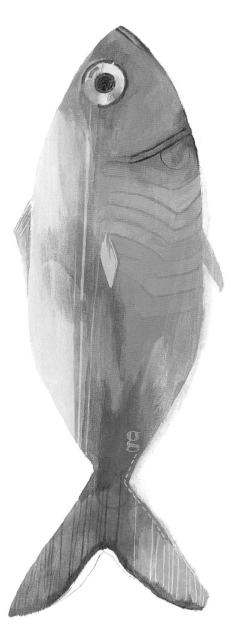

Cod, Fennel and Smoked Bacon Pie

Serves 6

just over 1kg boned, filleted cod (a good 2½cm thick), cut into 3 x 3cm chunks

4 fennel bulbs, the faintly stringy/woody layers removed then quartered vertically (see page 31)

3 slices of smoked back bacon, snipped into fine strips (don't use any more than 3 rashers or the pie will be overflavoured)

2 tablespoons finely chopped fresh flat leaf parsley

2 tablespoons finely snipped fresh chives

300ml béchamel sauce (see page 28)

900g potatoes, peeled, boiled then mashed with butter, milk, salt and pepper

butter, for dotting

salt and pepper

• Put the cod chunks in the bottom of a deep ovenproof dish. Season with salt and pepper.
• Steam the fennel quarters until just unresistant at their base. (If this term is too 'cooky'! – just spike their bums with a knife and they should be slightly soft.) Add them to the fish.
• Fry the bacon strips until browned in a small pan, drain and add to the fish and fennel.
• Add the herbs to the béchamel sauce when you have taken it off the heat. Pour over the fish. There may not look enough sauce, but the cod exudes juices.
• Cover the dish with mashed potato. Ruffle the surface with a fork and dot with butter.
• Cook in a preheated oven, 180°C/350°F/Gas 4, for 30–40 minutes, until browned and bubbling.

Baked Fish

Serves 1

To bake a fish you can't really go wrong, unless you are one of those culinary disaster zones and get seriously drunk on the wine you were supposed to be serving with the fish.

350g fish (such as plaice), gutted (the fishmonger's will do it for you)

handful of fresh parsley, chopped

1 lemon, sliced

• Stuff the gutted fish with some parsley and slices of lemon. (I buy the plaice whole and cook them on the bone – the amount of lemon and parsley will depend on the size of the fish)
• Place the fish on a large bit of foil and seal it into a parcel. Don't seal it too tight as the steam the fish gives off helps it cook faster. Place it in a roasting tin or on a baking sheet.
• Fish takes very little time to cook, I would give it a max of 30 minutes in a preheated oven at 180°C/350°F/Gas 4 – enough time to make a salad or prepare and cook some carrots to serve with it.

Pan-Fried Plaice with Lemon and Parsley

Serves 2

A fantastically quick and easy dish!

flour, for dusting
2 good-sized, spanking fresh plaice
50g butter
handful of fresh parsley, chopped
juice of ½ a lemon

• Sprinkle out enough flour to thinly cover a large plate.
• The plaice should be slippery wet. If it has been in the fridge for a couple of days, dip in a bit of milk first, before dipping it in the plate of flour.
• Melt most of the butter in a large shallow pan until it froths and bubbles, slide in the plaice and fry. You may have to cook one fish at a time, depending on the size of your pan, although the fish will shrink a little in the pan. Bubbles should frame the fish.
• Cook for 1 minute until golden underneath. Turn carefully and cook for a further 2 minutes. It won't need more than 3–4 minutes on each side, depending on the size of the fish. If the butter browns then turn the heat down. The fish should be golden brown on the outside, and the flesh white and wobbly underneath. Lift on to dinner plates.
• Tip out the used butter and add the remaining fresh butter to the pan. Let it froth and turn golden brown, but only just. Add the parsley and the lemon juice. Cook for 30 seconds then pour the contents of the pan over the fish and serve.
• This fish goes well with green beans and mashed potato – whatever takes your fancy!

Kedgeree
Serves 4–5

750g smoked haddock (this is one of the cheapest fish in a fishmonger's)
about 300ml milk
a little butter
500g rice
4 tablespoons olive oil
2 large onions, thinly sliced
1 clove garlic, finely chopped
4 eggs
225g fresh or frozen peas
large bunch of fresh parsley, finely chopped
salt and pepper

• Lay the fish in a gratin dish (like a Pyrex one). Pour over enough milk to cover, dot with butter, grind over some black pepper and put in a preheated oven, 180°C/350°F/Gas 4, for 15 minutes, until just tender.
• Meanwhile, add the rice to a saucepan of boiling water and add some salt. Stir and put the lid on. Cook until tender – it takes about 35–40 minutes. I always cook by the time it states in the packet, taste it and always burn my mouth so watch out!
• Twenty minutes before the rice is ready, heat the oil in a large heavy-bottomed frying pan. Add the onions and garlic. Cook over a low heat, stirring, for 2–3 minutes. Then put a lid on, turn down to the lowest heat possible and stew for 20 minutes.
• When the rice is cooked add it to the onions.
• When the fish is ready, flake it, removing the bones and skin, and reserve the poaching milk.
• Add the flaked fish to the rice and onions and add some of the milk and fish juices – not too much as you just need to keep it moist.
• Hard-boil the eggs. I cook the eggs and the peas together in the same pan to save on washing-up. The eggs should go into the boiling water first, after 5 minutes add the peas and cook for 8 minutes in total.
• Drain the peas and add to the kedgeree mixture. Shell the eggs.
• Take the kedgeree off the heat, add a bit more of the milk to stop it drying out. Sprinkle with parsley, and serve decorated with the halved boiled eggs and a little butter. Serve.

Fish Cakes

Serves 3

2 large potatoes, peeled and chopped

500g fish (such as salmon, cod, haddock, or haddock and smoked haddock together. Cod is cheap, but smoked haddock has a better flavour)

a little butter

2–4 tablespoons milk

chopped fresh parsley

1 egg, beaten

60g breadcrumbs

oil, for frying

salt and pepper

• Put the potatoes in a pan of cold water and boil for 15–20 minutes till soft.

• Put the fish in a Pyrex dish, dot with butter and sprinkle with salt and pepper. Add just enough milk to cover the fish. Bake in a preheated oven, 180°C/350°F/Gas 4, for about 20 minutes.

• Take the fish out and keep the milk. Flake the fish and set aside. Mash the potatoes, using the reserved milk and some butter.

• Add the fish to the mash with the parsley. Make four or five fish cakes. Roll them in the beaten egg, then straight in the breadcrumbs. Heat some oil in a frying pan and fry the fish cakes for 5–10 minutes on each side, until golden brown.

Who Ate All The Pies?

Pie munching is the pastime of many bored students. It can take place in the form of communal munchies after a huge drinking *fest* or in the legendary feasts that can be created from this book.

Pie-making usually triggers alarm bells: 'Oh no, I have to make pastry'. Believe me, it's not that hard and the end result, such as a hearty steak and kidney pie, is well worth the effort. If you can't face it, your local pub probably offers a good alternative, but I promise you, it won't taste as good as your own.

Chicken and Leek Pie

Serves 5

This recipe is dedicated to my bestest friend Jess, aka Dump, my eating partner in crime. We pie munch together through thick and thin.

1 whole chicken, about 1½kg
1 onion, left unpeeled
2 sticks celery, chopped
bouquet of fresh herbs
1 quantity shortcrust pastry (see page 111)
6 leeks, washed and sliced
2 tablespoons chopped fresh parsley
1 egg, beaten
salt and pepper

• Put the chicken in a large pan with the onion, celery, herbs and seasoning. Add enough water to cover the chicken and simmer until the chicken is cooked – about 45 minutes. Spike the chicken with a knife and pull back the flesh, it should be cream, not pink. Take the pan off the heat and leave to cool. Remove the chicken meat from the carcass. **Keep the cooking water.**

• Meanwhile, make the pastry according to the instructions on page 111 and put it in the fridge, or run to the supermarket and buy a packet of ready-made pastry (225g).

• Cook the leeks for 2 minutes in salted boiling water. (You can also cook carrots and potatoes, too, if you want more in your pie!)

• Grease a 24–26 cm pie dish and add the cooked vegetables.

• Dice the cooked chicken and add to the pie dish with the parsley and seasoning. Pour in enough stock from the boiled chicken pan to just cover. If you prefer a thicker sauce, add some cornflour to the stock and warm it over a low heat before pouring over the chicken and veg.

• Roll out the pastry on a lightly floured surface. Cut a strip and place it around the rim of the pie dish. Brush the pastry strip with beaten egg. Lay the main part of the pastry over the pie to make a lid and press the pastry edges together. Trim off the excess with a knife to neaten.

• Make a central hole for the steam to escape. (You can use a ceramic bird if you like! – this has a hole in its mouth through which it lets the steam out of the pie.)

• Brush the whole pie with beaten egg to give it a golden crispy look when cooked and to stop the pie crust drying out. Cook for 20–25 minutes in a preheated oven, 230°C/450°F/Gas 8, until the pastry is golden, then lower the heat to 180°C/350°F/Gas 4 and cook for a further 20 minutes.

Steak and Kidney Pie

Serves 6

Non-kidney lovers can use extra beef instead – so if you cook this for me you know what to do!

350g lamb's kidneys (…mmmm yum!)

750g steak, any fat or tough fibres removed then cut into chunks

5 x tablespoons olive oil

2 onions, finely chopped

1 clove garlic, crushed

2 carrots, peeled and thinly sliced

1 tablespoon plain white flour

375ml water

1 bay leaf

sprig of fresh thyme

sprig of fresh parsley

1 teaspoon Worcestershire sauce

225g button mushrooms, sliced

generous squeeze of lemon juice

1 quantity shortcrust pastry (see page 111)

½ egg, beaten with 2 tablespoons milk

salt and pepper

• Peel the fine membrane off the kidneys (rather you than me!), slice them in half and expose the tough white core inside. Using scissors, cut around each half core until cut out – better still, ask the butcher to do it for you. Dice the kidneys, and season both meats.

• Heat 4 tablespoons of the oil in a heavy-bottomed saucepan. Brown the beef and then the kidneys in separate batches. Remove them and set them aside on a plate.

• Lower the heat, add the onions, garlic and carrots and sauté for 5 minutes. Stir in the flour and cook for 1 more minute.

• Return the meat to the saucepan with the water, herbs and Worcestershire sauce. Bring to the boil, add pepper and salt and simmer very gently for 1½ hours. Remove the herb sprigs at the end of cooking.

• Heat the remaining oil in a small frying pan, and quickly colour the mushrooms. Add the lemon juice then mix into the meat stew. Season if it needs. Transfer the filling to a deep 24–26 cm pie dish. Allow the mixture to cool before putting the pastry on top.

• When ready to bake, roll out the pastry on a lightly floured surface to roughly the same shape as your pie dish but a bit larger. Cut a long strip from the edge of the pastry. Press it firmly around the rim of the pie dish and brush with a little of the egg and milk mixture.

• Place a ceramic bird (see page 57) in the middle of the meat filling. Roll the remaining pastry on to the rolling pin, then lift on to the pie dish over the filling to form the pie lid. Press the

pastry edges around the rim of the dish together firmly with a fork, and cut off the excess pastry with a knife to neaten.

• Prick with a knife and brush with more milk and egg. Ensure there is a hole for the steam to escape during cooking.

• Place the pie in the centre of a preheated oven, 220°C/425°F/Gas 7, and bake for 35 minutes, until the pastry has puffed up and turned golden.

Comfort Food

We all know how good this kind of food can make you feel. If you have had a bad day, are worrying about too many essays left until the last minute, you miss home, or you have a cold – which feels worse when mum isn't around to look after you – whip up one of these recipes and you will find that even the smells remind you of a yummy home memory.

Third Generation Chicken with Lemon

Serves 4

My legend of a grandma first fed me this, and it was then demanded every time I stayed with her! This is an easier version of her recipe.

4 teaspoons honey
4 chicken breasts, skinned
juice of 1 large orange
juice of ½ lemon
1 tablespoon soy sauce
125ml single cream (optional)
salt and pepper

• Rub a teaspoonful of honey into each chicken piece then lay them in a greased shallow baking dish.
• Mix together the orange and lemon juice, soy sauce, cream if using, and salt and pepper then pour over the chicken.
• Cover the dish with foil and bake in a preheated oven, 150°C/300°F/Gas 2, for 40 minutes. Take the foil off for the last couple of minutes and spoon some of the sauce over the top so the chicken breasts don't dry out!
• Serve with rice, potatoes or salad, or on its own. If you're feeling lazy just whack each piece between two hunks of bread and enjoy.

Bacon & Potato Hotpot

Serves 4

If you want its posh name, it's 'Pomme Dauphinoise with Bacon'.

4 large potatoes, peeled and sliced
4 large onions, finely chopped
225g bacon, rinded and chopped into small pieces
15g Cheddar cheese, grated
For the béchamel sauce:
45g butter
45g plain flour
375ml milk
salt and pepper

• Make a béchamel sauce by gently melting the butter in a saucepan. Add the flour and stir until it gets thick and bubbles. Let the mixture cook for a minute, stirring so that it doesn't burn. This is to take the taste of the flour away.
• Stir in the milk slowly over the lowest heat possible. You may need to use a whisk to avoid getting any lumps. Season with salt and pepper.
• Place the potato slices under cold running water for a couple of minutes to wash off the starch.
• Grease an ovenproof dish and layer it with the potatoes, then the bacon then the onions, repeating twice and then finishing with a layer of potatoes. Pour the béchamel sauce on top and sprinkle over the cheese.
• Bake for 1½ hours in the centre of a preheated oven, 180°C/350°F/Gas 4. Move the hotpot to the top shelf for the last 20 minutes.

Lamb Kebabs

Serves 4

500g boned lamb, cut into cubes
1 large onion, cut into chunks
4 tomatoes, cut into chunks
8 small mushrooms
2 peppers, cored, seeded and cut into chunks

For the marinade:
6 tablespoons olive oil
juice of 1 lemon
pinch of dried mixed herbs
soy sauce, to taste
salt and pepper

• Mix together the marinade ingredients.
• Soak the cubes of lamb in the marinade
for a couple of hours to tenderize the meat.
• Thread alternate pieces of lamb, onion,
tomato, mushrooms and peppers on to
8 skewers.
• Cook the kebabs in the oven at 180ºC,
or ideally on a barbecue, for 10 minutes,
until the meat is brown on the outside,
but still juicy on the inside.

Chicken with Barbecue Sauce

Serves 6

This barbecue sauce is famous in my house, and is actually my legend-of-a-mum's invention.

12 pieces of chicken (or spare ribs)

For the barbecue sauce:
125ml tomato ketchup
1 tablespoon soy sauce
1 tablespoon Worcestershire sauce
2 teaspoons cider vinegar
1 tablespoon olive oil
2 teaspoons tomato purée
2 teaspoons grainy mustard
1 tablespoon honey
2 teaspoons molasses sugar or dark brown muscovado sugar
juice of 1 small orange
3 cloves garlic, crushed
2½cm square piece of fresh root ginger, crushed
salt and pepper

• Mix all the barbecue sauce ingredients together well in a bowl to make a marinade.
• Put the chicken pieces (or spare ribs) in a roasting tin, pour over the marinade and leave for 1 hour.
• Cover the tin with foil and bake in a preheated oven, 180°C/350°F/Gas 4, for 30 minutes.
• After 30 minutes remove the foil and cook uncovered for 5–10 minutes. Test the meat with a knife – it should be pale and tender, not pink.

Carry on cooking for a further 5 minutes if it needs it, if not take it out of the oven and eat.
• Serve with rice. Alternatively, mashed potato and peas is a craving of mine with this sauce – I can't get enough of it!

Chicken Stew

Serves 4

This recipe goes really well with Couscous

6 chicken legs
1 onion
2 cloves of garlic, crushed
olive oil for frying
Knob of butter
stock (see page 13)
8 tomatoes
2 sticks celery, chopped
1 tin of whole tomatoes with their juice
salt and pepper.

• Chop the onion in half and slice into thin strips
• Heat oil and a knob of butter in a pan and add
the onion, garlic and celery, frying gently.
• Add the chicken legs and stir until coated in
the oil.
• Add enough stock to cover and bring it to the
boil.
• Whilst waiting for it to start bubbling, boil a
kettle and put the water in a large bowl. Cross
the bottoms of the tomatoes with a knife and put
in the boiling water until the skin starts to
separate from the flesh. Throw away the hot
water and run cold water over them. Peel the
skin off, quarter them and remove the seeds.
Chop into chunks.
• Add the tinned tomatoes and juice, the
chopped fresh tomatoes and salt and pepper.
Simmer slowly for up to an hour, on a low heat
with the lid on - allowing the sauce to thicken as
it cooks

Mozzarella Meatballs

Serves 4

250g lean organic minced beef

1 small onion, finely chopped

1 teaspoon chopped fresh parsley

1 egg, beaten
½ mozzarella cheese

Wholemeal flour, for coating

3 tablespoons olive oil

pepper, to taste

For the sauce:

1 teaspoon olive oil
½ onion, finely chopped

1 garlic clove, crushed

1 celery stick, finely chopped

5 tomatoes, skinned, de-seeded and chopped

1 teaspoon tomato purée

1 teaspoon molasses sugar

pepper, to taste

• To make the meatball, put the beef, onion, herbs and beaten egg in a bowl and mix well, adding pepper to taste.

• Cut the mozzarella into ¾ inch (2cm) cubes and mould the meat mixture around each one. Roll the meatballs in flour to coat.

• Heat the olive oil in a frying pan and fry the meatballs for 12–13 minutes or until cook through and browned.

• To make the sauce, heat the olive oil in a saucepan. Add the onion, garlic and the celery and cook gently for about 6 minutes or until soft. Add the remaining ingredients, with pepper to taste, and continue cooking gently until the sauce is pulpy.

• Serve the meatballs on top of boiled spaghetti sprinkled with Parmesan cheese, with the hot sauce spooned over the top.

Broccoli and Chicken Gratin

Serves 4

½ roasted chicken (the other half of Sunday lunch)

500g broccoli, cut into florets

450ml béchamel sauce (see page 28, but note you need to increase the quantities)

450ml chicken stock (see page 13)

1 heaped teaspoon dried tarragon

4–6 tablespoons dry white wine

2 heaped tablespoons Parmesan cheese, grated

50g breadcrumbs

1 heaped tablespoon butter, melted

6 tablespoons double cream

freshly grated nutmeg

salt and pepper

• Remove the meat from the chicken carcass and arrange in the base of a greased ovenproof dish. (**Remember you can use the chicken bones to make stock, see page 13**.)

• Cook the broccoli in a saucepan of boiling water for 4 minutes. Drain and add to the chicken in the dish.

• Boil down the béchamel sauce in a saucepan with the stock and tarragon. Add the wine and season to taste with salt, pepper and nutmeg.

• Take the sauce off the heat – the consistency should be thick – and add the cheese and cream gradually. Pour over the chicken and broccoli.

• Scatter the breadcrumbs on top. Pour the melted butter over the breadcrumbs.

• Bake the gratin in a preheated oven, 180°C/ 350°F/Gas 4, until the gratin bubbles at the edges and the chicken has had a chance to heat through. Check after 10–15 minutes – it should be looking golden. If not, cook for another 5 minutes or so, but **don't let it burn**.

Toad in the Hole

Serves 4

Believe it or not, you can make toad in the hole a bit more extravagant with a browned onion and Madeira gravy. Sounds a bit fancy, but it's easy to make, and you can do it while the batter is in the oven.

2 eggs

125g plain flour

150ml milk mixed with 150ml cold water

1 level teaspoon wholegrain mustard

6 thick pork sausages (herby ones if you're splashing out, if not cheapies are cool)

6 rashers of bacon

3 tablespoons olive oil

salt and pepper

For the gravy:

75g butter

2 large onions, thinly sliced

1 tablespoon plain flour

250ml stock

75ml red wine

Worcestershire sauce, to taste

• To make the batter, mix the eggs, flour, milk and water, mustard and some salt and pepper together with a whisk, beating out any little lumps of flour as you go. The consistency should be like double cream. Leave to rest for 15 minutes.

• Cut then peel the skin off each sausage and wrap each skinned sausage in a bacon rasher.

• Put the oil in a 28 x 21cm baking tin and place in a preheated oven, 220°C/425°F/Gas 7, until steaming. Take out after 3–4 minutes and pour in the batter. It will sizzle softly in the hot fat.

• Arrange the sausages in the batter. Put in the oven and bake for 25–30 minutes, till the batter is puffed and golden.

• To make the gravy, melt the butter in a heavy-bottomed pan, add the onions and cook over a low heat till golden and soft.

• Add the flour and continue cooking for a few minutes until it has lightly browned, then pour in the stock and red wine. Season with salt, pepper and Worcestershire sauce and bring to the boil.

• Turn the heat down so the gravy bubbles gently and leave for about 15 minutes, stirring from time to time.

Savoury Pancakes

Serves 4–5

There are two different fillings for these pancakes here – leek and bacon or spinach and cheese.

For the basic pancake mixture:

225g plain flour
pinch of salt
2 eggs
500ml milk
butter to grease the pan

For the leek and bacon filling:

5 leeks (white part only), washed and chopped
5 rashers of bacon, chopped
300ml béchamel sauce (see page 28)
30g Cheddar cheese, grated

• Sift the flour and salt into a big mixing bowl.

• Make a 'well' in the flour and break the eggs into it. Whisk the ingredients together, drawing in the flour from the sides.

• Add the milk, bit by bit. Beat until the mixture is smooth, and thick enough to coat a wooden spoon.

• To make pancakes, the frying pan needs to be the right temperature and have the right amount of butter. If the pan is steaming the temperature is too high. Use a small knob of butter, melt it gently and then add a couple of tablespoons of pancake mixture. Swoosh it around the frying pan to cover the bottom. Flip the pancake when the mixture begins to bubble in the middle. We have a rule in my house that the first one never works so don't get ratty and give up.

• Continue making pancakes, one at a time, until the mixture is all used up.

• To make the leek and bacon filling, steam or boil the leeks, and fry the chopped bacon in a frying pan. Place a line of leeks and bacon down the middle of each pancake.

• Roll up the pancakes and arrange them side by side in a small baking tin.

• Pour the béchamel sauce over the pancakes and cover with grated cheese.

• Bake in a preheated oven, 180°C/350°F/Gas 4, for 20 minutes – the cheese should be bubbling and golden.

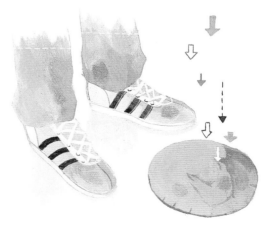

Variation:

For the spinach and cheese filling:
900g spinach
1 onion, finely chopped
25g butter
2 tablespoons plain white flour
675g tomatoes, finely chopped
3 tablespoons tomato purée
2 garlic cloves, crushed
1 vegetable stock cube
100g Cheddar cheese, grated
salt and pepper

• Rinse the spinach several times under running water and remove any tough stems. Chop roughly then cook the spinach briefly (without water) for about 3 minutes in a pan with a tightly fitting lid. Spinach has a high water content so the water left on the leaves from washing is sufficient to cook it. **Stir** and **don't let the pan dry out**, as burnt spinach is grim.
• To make the sauce, cook the chopped onion in the butter until translucent. Stir in the flour, then cook for 1 further minute.
• Add the finely chopped tomatoes to the onion mixture and stir over the heat until the sauce boils and thickens.
• Then add the tomato purée and garlic, stock cube and a little salt and pepper. Simmer gently over a medium heat for 2 minutes.

• Stir in the cheese and allow to melt.
• Add three-quarters of the sauce to the cooked spinach. Divide the mixture between the pancakes and roll up.
• Place the pancakes in a greased ovenproof dish, spoon over the remaining sauce and bake at 180°C/350°F/Gas 4 for 20–30 minutes.

Roast Dinner

A roast dinner is one of the first things I learnt how to cook. Yes, it is quite difficult to time everything exactly to the 'T', but after a few attempts it sticks in your head and you can just get on with it.

The meat always goes in first, at around eleven o'clock on a Sunday in our house. The vegetables get peeled – potatoes and parsnips are quite happy sitting in a pan of water until you are ready to parboil them. I parboil them at the same time the meat goes in. Remember to put a couple of oiled baking trays in the oven to get hot – but not for too long as they start spitting.

Drain the potatoes and parsnips and then put them straight on to the trays and in the oven. They take nearly the same amount of time as the meat to crisp up and cook through.

Once peeled and chopped, vegetables such as carrots, broccoli, sprouts are fine in water, too, and need about half an hour before you take the meat out. This allows you a bit of time for a shower and a few bloody Marys to cure the old hangover before tucking into a nice lunch!

Cooking Times and Temperatures

Things to remember:

• Take meat out of the fridge or freezer in good time.

• I always cook game birds breast down first.

• Baste meat at all times. This means keep spooning over the juice the joint is cooking in so that the top doesn't dry out and it crisps up, as the juice is mostly fat. **This needs to be done to all meats.**

• A normal beef joint size feeds four people.

Cooking times

Gas Mark	°C	°F	Description	Gas Mark	°C	°F	Description
1	140	275	very cool	6	200	400	fairly hot
2	150	300	cool	7	220	425	hot
3	160	325	warm	8	230	450	very hot
4	180	350	moderate	9	240	475	very hot
5	190	375	fairly hot				

Starting oven temperature	After 15 minutes	Minutes per 500g
Beef – 240°C/475°F/Gas 9	180°C/350°F/Gas 4	Rare 15 mins
		Medium 18 mins
		Well done 25 mins
Chicken – 200°C/400°F/Gas 6	200°C/400°F/Gas 6	20 minutes + 30 overall per 500g
Duck – 220°C/425°F/Gas 7	180°C/350°F/Gas 4	20 minutes per 500g
Goose – 200°C/400°F/Gas 6	200°C/400°F/Gas 6	15 minutes + 30 overall per 500g
Lamb – 240°C/475°F/Gas 9	200°C/400°F/Gas 6	Rare 12 minutes per 500g
		Medium 16 minutes per 500g
		Well done 20 minutes per 500g
Pork – 200°C/400°F/Gas 6	180°C/350°F/Gas 4	30 minutes per 500g
Veal – 220°C/425°F/Gas 7	180°C/350°F/Gas 4	20 minutes per 500g

Turkey (with stuffing included)

Weight	Time	
2.25kg	1½ hours	Rub skin with butter, cover with foil
4.5kg	2 hours	and cook at 200°C/400°F/Gas 6 for
6.75kg	2¾ hours	45 mins, Remove foil, turn down to
9kg	3½ hours	180°C/350°F/Gas 4 and keep basting
11.5kg	4½ hours	for the rest of the cooking time.

Chestnut Stuffing

Serves 4–5

Please don't look at the word shallots (it's a type of small onion) and chestnuts and think 'too adventurous'. It tastes wicked and takes only 10–15 minutes to prepare.

75g butter
175g shallots, finely chopped
75g smoked streaky bacon, rinded and chopped
2 eggs, beaten
435g tin unsweetened chestnut purée
200g tin or vacuum pack whole chestnuts, roughly chopped
200g fresh breadcrumbs
bunch of fresh parsley, finely chopped
freshly grated nutmeg
salt and pepper

• Melt the butter and cook the shallots with the bacon for about 10 minutes over a low heat or until soft and beginning to colour.
• Add the beaten eggs to the chestnut purée.
• Add the roughly chopped chestnuts to the egg purée with the breadcrumbs, shallots and bacon and chopped parsley. Add salt and pepper and a good grating of nutmeg.
• Stuff the turkey, goose or chicken.

Yorkshire Pudding

Serves 4–5

Make this in a single large baking dish, it's easier than using the fussy little muffin trays.

112g flour
pinch of salt
1 egg
250ml milk

• Sift the flour and mix with the salt. Make a 'well' in the centre and break the egg into it.
• Add a little milk and starting in the middle of the bowl, use a whisk to stir the ingredients into a batter – gradually pouring in the remaining milk as you whisk.
• Leave the batter to rest for 20 minutes while you carry on with making the rest of the dinner like peeling the vegetables, then put into a preheated oven, 200°C/400°F/Gas 6, for 25–30 minutes. Drain off the fat at the end.

Crunchy Roast Potatoes and Parsnips

potatoes (2–3 per person)
parsnips (1 per person)
4 tablespoons olive oil

• Peel and chop the potatoes to a decent size. Generally, I cook 2–3 potatoes and 1 parsnip per person.
• Slice any large potatoes in half. Also halve the parsnips. Put them in a pan of cold water and bring to the boil. Boil for 5–10 minutes.
• During this time heat two roasting tins, each with a couple of tablespoons of olive oil in.
• Drain the potatoes and parsnips (keep the cooking water in a jug for the gravy – see right).
• Ruffle the potatoes with a fork or in a metal colander to loosen the outsides slightly. This makes them go really crispy and yummy when cooked. Put them in the tins with the hot oil.
• Put the potatoes and parsnips in the oven at around the same time the meat goes in. You can put the meat in first, depending on how long you have to cook the meat for – potatoes and parsnips need 45 minutes to 1 hour at 200°C/400°F/Gas 6. If you want to save on washing-up and are not cooking for the hoards in halls, place them around the meat and cook in the same roasting tin.
• Remember to keep turning the potatoes and parsnips every 10–15 minutes, and if they are not crispy towards the end, move them to the top of the oven and move the meat down.

Gravy from the Pan Juices

I hope Bisto – which is supposedly easier when you are trying to do a hundred things like vegetables, stuffing, meat and potatoes, all at the same time – is not the first thing to spring to mind. This recipe is so easy and uses the meat juices left in the pan after the chicken or meat is cooked. I promise they are the best starter for a good gravy.
I like my plate swimming in gravy, while Tom likes his food dry.

roast juices from the tin
dash of wine
cornflour, to thicken (optional)

• Turn a ring on the hob low, and put the whole roasting tin, with the roast juices still in it, over the heat.
• Add a dash of wine if you can bear to part with it and a dessert spoon of cornflour to thicken it if you want.
• Add the water drained off from the boiled potatoes or vegetables, and simmer the gravy for 2–3 minutes. You may have to whisk it if the cornflour is a bit lumpy.

Brussels Sprouts

• To cook Brussels sprouts, boil them in salted water for 3–5 minutes. **Don't forget to cross the bottoms** with a knife – this helps them to cook.

Leeks in Parsley sauce

4–5 leeks, chopped
1 tablespoon of butter
1 tablespoon of flour
1 tablespoon chopped parsley
125ml milk (approx)

• Chop the leeks into thin rings and boil until soft. Drain.
• Add the butter to the saucepan and stir gently while it melts, trying not to break the leeks up too much.
• Add the flour and stir in the milk slowly. It will thicken around the leeks. Do not add all the milk at once – you may not need to use it all!
• Add the tablespoon of parsley... and there you go!

Roasted Onions

• Roast one onion per person. Leave them whole, in the skin and roast them around the meat (or wrap separately in foil).

Vegetables and Vegetarian

Some make you less than pleasant to be around, most stop constipation, and they are cheap and easy to cook. Usually no one can be arsed with vegetables when there are tins of baked beans and frozen peas as a very good alternative. Believe me, I am never one to turn down baked beans on toast or frozen peas – they rule, but they are not very nutritious and they can get boring.

So, get off your arse and go to the supermarket or greengrocer's. Vegetables are no more or no less work to put in a pan than to cook a ready-made meal. Never overcook vegetables as you will lose loads of vitamins, and you may as well have opened a tin or dipped your hand in the freezer.

Cauliflower Cheese

Serves 4

You can omit the bacon in this recipe if you are a veggie!

1 large cauliflower
2 tablespoons olive oil
1 small onion, diced
8 slices of bacon (optional)
2–3 tomatoes (optional)
300ml cheese sauce (see page 28 – use 200g grated Cheddar cheese, keep some by for the top)

• Cut away the leaves from the cauliflower. Turn upside down and cut around the stem to remove the cone-shaped core. Gently pull the florets apart and wash thoroughly in cold water.
• Bring a large saucepan of salted water to the boil. Boil the cauliflower for 5 minutes or until just tender then drain immediately using a colander.
• Heat the oil in a frying pan over a moderate heat and fry the onion until soft.
• Trim the fat off the bacon and dice. Add the bacon to the onions and fry until just cooked.
• If using tomatoes, cut them into eighths, removing the cores.
• Arrange the florets in a gratin dish, sprinkle over the onions and bacon and tomatoes.
• Pour over the cheese sauce. At this stage the dish can be chilled until you feel like heating it up, just clingfilm it and refrigerate.
• When ready to cook, sprinkle the remaining grated Cheddar cheese on top. Cook in a preheated oven, 220°C/425°F/Gas 7, for 15–20 minutes – **it should be bubbling hot** and the cheese golden.

Tip: You could make this dish larger by cooking pasta in the cauliflower water and adding it to the dish before the cheese sauce.

Red Hot Broccoli

Serves 4

olive oil, for frying
2 dried red chillies
½ sweet red pepper, cored, seeded and
roughly chopped
500g broccoli (or 1 cauliflower), cut into florets
1 tablespoon soy sauce (optional)

• Pour out enough olive oil to cover the bottom
of your frying pan.
• Chop up the chillies and seed them. **Do not
then rub your eyes, bite your fingernails or pick
your nose!**
• Heat the oil gently for about 10 minutes with
the red pepper and chillies in it.
• Raise the heat to moderate, add the broccoli.
Stir with your great wooden Chinese frying
spatula from the jumble sale. The veg should
stew, not fry – it must not colour. Add the soy
sauce if not juicy enough
• Drain away the excess oil and place the veg
including the chillies and the pepper, in a dish,
then eat!

Broccoli with Eggs

Serves 2–3

**Useless fact to impress your friends: this is
apparently a favourite with English people since
the 18th century, when Italian broccoli was first
imported into Britain.**

500g broccoli, cut into florets
4 slices of bread
115g butter
dash of milk
6 eggs, beaten
salt and pepper

• Steam or boil the broccoli for 10 minutes.
• Trim the bread to fit in a serving dish. Toast it
on both sides and put in the dish to keep warm.
• Melt the butter in a saucepan, add the milk,
eggs and seasoning. Scramble the mixture by
stirring constantly until it starts to turn fluffy and
the eggs begin to set. **Don't overcook** as the
mixture carries on cooking off the heat.
• Pile the eggs on to the toast. Make a 'well' in
the middle and put the broccoli in it.
• If you want to make it more exciting you could
make the red hot broccoli.

Yummy Carrots

Serves 4

I want to dedicate this recipe to my friend Lou the bimbo, whose Dad left her a note to boil the carrots that were in a bag in the fridge, so she did just that – boiled them in the bag!

8 carrots, peeled and cut into thin fingers
a good chunk of butter
2 tablespoons dark brown muscovado sugar

• Put the carrots in a pan and add a small amount of water – it should not cover the carrots, the level should be below the carrots.
• Put the large chunk of butter on top and a good sprinkling of sugar.
• Boil all the water off, add more if the carrots aren't cooked. They should end up glazed by the butter and sugar and tasting good.

Mashed Carrot and Swede

Serves 4

1 swede, peeled and chopped into 2cm cubes
6 carrots, peeled and chopped into 2cm cubes
40g butter
dash of milk
salt and pepper

• Boil the swede and carrots together in a saucepan of boiling salted water for 20–30 minutes or until very tender.
• Mash in the saucepan with large amounts of butter and a small dash of milk.
• Season with salt and pepper and serve.

My Dad's Mash

Serves 3–4

6 medium potatoes, peeled, boiled
1 tablespoon olive oil
1 tablespoon milk
2 tablespoons butter
salt and pepper

• Boil the potatoes in a large saucepan until
cooked through.
• Put in a bowl and mash, adding the butter,
olive oil, milk, salt and pepper.
• If the mixture looks dry add a tiny bit of milk at
a time and stir until you reach the right
consistency.

Creamy Mashed Potato with Spring Onion

Serves 3–4

900g potatoes, peeled, boiled then mashed
with butter, milk, salt and pepper
3–4 spring onions, finely chopped
4 rashers bacon, finely chopped (optional, for non-
veggies)
Cheddar cheese (or Parmesan cheese
if you have it), grated
HP sauce, to taste (optional)
salt and pepper

• Make a bowl of hot mashed potato (see
previous recipe).
• Fry the spring onion (and bacon if using it) in a
little olive oil until golden. Mix in with the potato
• Turn the potato into a Pyrex dish and spread
until even.
Sprinkle over some grated cheese. A good friend
of mine swears by HP sauce, which you can also
sprinkle on top with the cheese.
• Cook in a preheated oven, 120°C/250°F/Gas ½
for 10–15 minutes, until the cheese is melted
and golden brown.

Spinach and Potato Omelette
Serves 4

1 onion, chopped
2 cloves garlic, chopped
2 tablespoons olive oil
4 small boiled potatoes, diced
225g spinach
4 eggs
pinch of salt
chopped fresh parsley
grated cheese (optional)

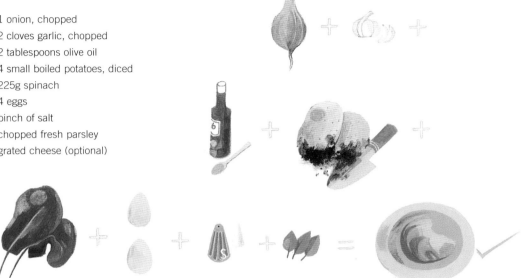

• Fry the onion and garlic in the oil in a large omelette pan or frying pan until translucent.

• Add the diced potato and cook until everything becomes a soft, 'mushy' mess.

• Rinse the spinach several times under running water, shake well and cook over a low heat, in a pan with a tightly fitting lid, for about 3 minutes. There should be no need to add any water. Spinach has a high water content and the water that remains on the leaves after washing is sufficient for cooking it.

• Drain the spinach in a colander by pressing the water out with a saucer. Chop it finely then add to the omelette pan.

• Beat the eggs with a pinch of salt, add the cheese and chopped parsley and pour into the pan.

• Move the vegetables about with a wooden spatula so that the egg completely covers the bottom of the pan. Cook gently over a medium/low heat until the underside is brown. Then turn over and finsh off by cooking for a minute on the other side.

Stuffed Tomatoes

Serves 6

**These can also be stuffed with bolognese sauce
(see page 26)**

6 large, firm tomatoes
450g spinach
60g butter
2 cloves garlic, crushed
3 tablespoons pine nuts
salt and pepper

• Cut the tops off the tomatoes. Carefully scoop out the pulp and discard.
• Rinse the spinach several times under running water, shake well and cook for 7–10 minutes in just the water adhering to its leaves, in a tightly covered pan. Do not overcook the spinach.
• Drain the spinach in a colander by pressing the water out with a saucer then chop very finely or put through a food processor to reduce to a purée. Add half the butter and season with salt and pepper and crushed garlic.
• Fry the pine nuts in the remaining butter, stirring all the time until they are crisp and light brown.
• Drain and add to the spinach purée, mix well then spoon into the tomato cases.
• Cook in a preheated oven, 180°C/350°F/Gas 4, for 20–30 minutes or until heated through. The tomatoes should be just hot and not soft. Serve immediately.

Ratatouille

Serves 8–10

The ingredients for this recipe can be adjusted to availability. Ratatouille can be eaten hot or cold or reheated, used in a vegetable lasagne, on top of pasta or in a jacket potato. I find it's particularly good with grilled meat.

500g aubergines, peeled and sliced

500g courgettes, peeled and sliced

4 tablespoons olive oil

2 large cloves garlic, chopped

3 large onions, sliced

3 sweet peppers (one of each colour for contrast if you like), cored, seeded and cut into strips

500g skinned tomatoes (tinned whole ones or skin fresh ones yourself with the boiling water trick – see page 9), roughly chopped

sugar, to taste

1 teaspoon vinegar

¼ teaspoon coriander seeds, crushed

9 leaves fresh basil, hand torn into small bits or parsley, chopped

salt and pepper

• Put the aubergines and courgettes in a colander, sprinkle with 1 teaspoon salt and leave for 1 hour to drain. When the hour is up, pat them dry with kitchen paper.

• Heat the oil and garlic in a large pan, then add the sliced onions and cook slowly, without browning. As the onions soften, add the aubergines and peppers. Cover and simmer for 20 minutes.

• After 20 minutes, add the tomatoes and courgettes. Season with salt, pepper and a little sugar and vinegar – no more than a teaspoon. Cook steadily until all the wateriness has disappeared – about 50 minutes.

• Ten minutes before the end of cooking, add the coriander seeds, basil and parsley. Try not to crush the veg too much when stirring – they should retain some sort of identity.

Tip: This can be served as I suggested above. If you are using the ratatouille to make lasagne, which is yummy, remember while the juice is boiling off you need to make a béchamel sauce (see page 28).

Spicy Couscous

Serves 3–4

Couscous can be very dry, so I suggest you use it like rice and serve something with it like marinated pork or fish. Unlike rice, it needs much less water to cook in and it's much quicker, too.

200g couscous
15ml oil
350ml boiling water
2 cloves garlic, finely chopped
1 onion, finely chopped
1 green pepper, cored, seeded and cut into strips
1 red pepper, cored, seeded and cut into strips
60g frozen peas
1 teaspoon paprika
salt and pepper

• Place the couscous in a large saucepan, season well and add a dash of the oil. Pour over the boiling water and leave to stand for 5 minutes.
• Put the remaining olive oil in a large saucepan. Heat the oil, and fry the garlic and onion for 2 minutes over a high heat.
• Add the peppers and stir. Immediately add the couscous, stir and then add the frozen peas. Cook for a further 4–5 minutes, taste to check the seasoning then serve.

Cheese, Leek and Spinach Quiche

Serves 6

pastry for a 20cm tart (see page 111)
300ml double cream
125g Gruyère cheese (or you can use cheddar!)
350g leeks
200g frozen, chopped spinach, thawed and squeezed dry
3 medium eggs
salt and pepper

• Make shortcrust pastry for a 20cm tart.
• Pre-heat the oven to 200°C/400°F/Gas 6.
• Chop up the leeks and rinse if they are dirty. Get rid of any tough bits and cook in butter until soft but not brown.
• Mix the cream, eggs and half the cheese in a bowl until blended.
• Spoon the leeks, spinach and the rest of the cheese into the pastry case. Top with the egg mixture.
• Bake the quiche for 25–30 minutes until the mixture is set and the top is browned.

Salads **My brother's favourite!**

No they are not filling, but they are healthy if you feel like you have killed every vitamin in your body after smoking, drinking and hard partying.

Salads can be eaten with almost anything, as you would know if you stayed at my place during the summer, where it's a daily tradition! I hate iceberg lettuce and little gems, but they're cheap so you will soon get used to them!

Dressing

There are loads of dressing variations. I recommend you experiment with amounts until you make one you like. This is the method I use.

1 teaspoon balsamic vinegar

1 teaspoon mustard (all mustards are good – I usually use Dijon if I want a bit of heat, or a seedy wholegrain mustard which you can easily find in the supermarket)

4 tablespoons olive oil

squeeze of lemon juice (optional)

salt and pepper

• I use an old jam jar and first add no more than a teaspoon of balsamic vinegar – if you use too much vinegar you will have to add a lot of oil
• Add the mustard to the vinegar and stir vigorously with a fork, then slowly add the olive oil, still stirring. Taste after a couple of tablespoons and add more oil if needed. If it's not strong enough, squeeze in a bit of lemon and add some pepper and salt to taste.

Variations: Try adding one of the following to the basic recipe above:
• Pinch of molasses sugar (dark brown).
• 1 clove of crushed garlic.
• 1 teaspoon natural yogurt
• Cider vinegar instead of balsamic vinegar (you don't need much as it's very strong)
• Wine vinegar, or a little of both balsamic and wine vinegar.
• Lemon juice instead of vinegar.

Odd Salad Dressing

This is good with the Bean Salad (see page 89).

2 eggs

250ml olive oil

1 tablespoon lemon juice

1 tablespoon chopped fresh parsley

1 clove garlic, crushed

• Hard-boil 2 eggs and crumble into a bowl.
• Gradually beat in the olive oil, lemon juice, chopped parsley and crushed garlic.

Tomato Salad

Serves 2–4

4 ripe tomatoes, sliced
olive oil, for drizzling
fresh basil leaves, torn (optional)
2 balls of mozzarella cheese, sliced (optional)
salt and pepper

• Tomatoes taste great just sprinkled with olive oil and some salt and pepper. Add a few torn basil leaves for flavour if your tomatoes taste a bit watery.
• You can also add sliced mozzarella cheese if you are feeling adventurous – and rich! Choose the type that comes in a bag preserved in water.

Tip: Something to remember is that tomatoes can have quite thick and bitter skins. To avoid this, spike with a knife, whack them in boiling water for a few seconds, let the skins loosen and then peel them.

Steamed Fennel Salad

Serves 4
Steamed fennel is yummy in a green bean and avocado salad.

2 fennel bulbs
2 avocadoes, stone removed and flesh sliced
500g green beans, lightly cooked
dressing of your choice (see page 87)
1 orange, peeled and thinly sliced (optional)

• Cut the fennel bulb lengthways into segments about 2cm thick. If you don't have a steamer, put the segments in a saucepan and add enough water to just cover the bottom of the pan. Bring to the boil, reduce the heat, cover and simmer for 20–25 minutes or until the fennel is tender.
• Serve with some sliced avocado, green beans and a dressing of your choice.
• It sounds weird, but thinly sliced orange goes really well in this salad, too.

Grated Carrot Salad

Grated carrot tastes fantastic with freshly squeezed lemon juice (I will kill you if you use Jiff!), a drizzle of olive oil and a little salt and pepper.

Bean Salad

This is a good simple salad. Just boil some green beans in water for 5–10 minutes (not to death – just until *al dente*) then throw a dressing of your choice over the top – try the Odd Salad Dressing (see page 87).

Home-Made Mayo

Makes 300ml

You will probably make this only once or twice when feeling creative and motivated. It really isn't very time-consuming and is good wrist exercise! It's really good mashed in with tuna, or with boiled potatoes in a potato salad (see page 91).

1 teaspoon mustard powder
1 egg yolk
300ml olive oil
juice of 1 lemon
salt and pepper

• Using a fork, beat the mustard powder with the egg yolk.
• With a wooden spoon, stir very well while **adding the oil very slowly**, practically drop-by-drop. If you add the oil too fast and don't stir fast enough **it will curdle** and you will most likely have to waste it and start again. Stop adding oil when the mixture is thick and pale.
• Add the lemon juice, while still stirring. Check the taste then add some salt and pepper. Chill and serve.

Greek-Style Cucumber

Serves 4 as a side salsd

I have just discovered that tzatziki is the real name of this Greek dish!

125g Greek yogurt or 125ml soured cream
1 clove garlic, crushed
small handful of fresh chives, chopped
small handful of fresh mint, chopped
1 cucumber, peeled and thinly sliced

• Mix together the yogurt, garlic and chives.
• Add the chopped mint to the yogurt dressing then pour over the cucumber.

Potato Salad
Serves 4–5

6 medium-sized potatoes, peeled and halved

handful of fresh herbs such as chives or parsley, chopped

4–5 tablespoons good mayonnaise like Hellmann's (or make you own if you have time – see page 90)

- Put the potatoes in a large saucepan of water and boil for 20–30 minutes or until soft. Spike with a knife to check.
- Drain off the water and let the potatoes cool. Then chop into 2cm chunks and put in a bowl.
- Stir the herbs into the mayonnaise. Add the mayonnaise to the potatoes and stir gently to coat. You might need a bit more mayonnaise depending on how thick you like the salad.

Salad Niçoise
Serves 4–5

2–3 green lettuces

handful of French beans, lightly cooked

handful of mangetout, lightly cooked

1 punnet baby/cherry tomatoes, sliced

5–6 tablespoons olive oil

2 x 250g tuna steaks, grilled quickly on both sides then flaked, or 6 small tins tuna, drained and flaked

10–12 new potatoes, boiled

5 hard-boiled eggs, shelled and halved

- Wash and thoroughly dry the lettuce then put in a large salad bowl.
- Add the beans, peas, tomatoes and olive oil. Using your fingers, gently turn the salad until everything is coated with oil.
- Add all the other ingredients and, again using your fingers, carefully mix them together. If you want it to look really flash, serve with the egg halves on the top to decorate.

Feta Cheese Salad

Serves 3–4

100g feta cheese, cubed
½ cucumber, sliced or cut into chunks
A handful of black olives
baby or 3 big tomatoes, sliced or cut into chunks
Small lettuce, washed
handful of fresh herbs, preferably thyme (use 1 teaspoon dried mixed herbs if you don't have fresh)

• Throw everything together in a big bowl, make it look pretty – or at least edible! – and serve. It's good with some bread, ham and cheese, and any other nibbles you may have in mind.

Tip: You can buy feta cheese in jars, preserved in olive oil with herbs. I keep the olive oil and use it for the dressing in another salad!

Walnut and Roquefort Salad

Serves 3–4

150g roquefort, cubed or crumbled with your fingers
a couple of handfuls of chopped walnuts
a small lettuce, washed
1 teaspoon cider vinegar
1 teaspoon brown sugar
4–5 teaspoons olive oil
1 teaspoon dijon mustard
a handful of freshly chopped chives

• Put the lettuce in a bowl and sprinkle the roquefort and walnuts over the top.
• To make the dressing put the mustard, vinegar and sugar in a bowl and stir in the oil slowly until you get the right consistency.
• Add the freshly chopped coriander and stir it in right before you add it to the salad.

Extravagant Extras

These recipes, which were demanded by Tom, are for when you are a bit more cocky with the old frying pan and recipe-reading technique and want to impress your *chica* or *chico*!

Guacamole

Serves 4

While travelling in South and Central America, I discovered the best way to eat guacamole is when you have the munchies with tortilla chips or plain tortillas, which are like pancakes. Spread over the guacamole, add a sprinkling of cheese and put them in a warm oven for 5 minutes. Take out, serve with a dollop of soured cream on top and then eat. Delicious!

2 cloves garlic, peeled and sliced

½ red onion, quartered

2 small red chillies, halved and seeded

5–6 ripe avocados, stones removed and peeled

2 large ripe tomatoes, skinned and finely chopped (see page 9)

juice of 2–4 limes (but taste as you add – don't just whack it all in! The limes stop the avocados from going brown)

few drops of Tabasco sauce (optional)

salt and pepper

chopped fresh coriander, to garnish

• Finely chop the garlic, onion and chillies until nearly a pulp. Perseverance is required, as it can take a while to get it tiny. Alternatively, you can just hurl them all in a food processor (if you have one), but this makes it too slimy for my taste. If you use a potato masher you will get a nice smooth, but not pulped, consistency.

• Mash the avocados to a pale paste. I tend to use a potato masher and leave some small chunks – I'll leave the decision to you.

• Add the garlic, onion and chillies to the avocados, along with the finely chopped tomatoes, lime juice and a few drops of Tabasco sauce if you like a bit of heat.

• Season with salt and pepper. Put the guacamole in a serving bowl, cover with clingfilm and chill until needed. Sprinkle chopped coriander on top before serving.

Potted Crab

Makes 12 ramekins

This recipe is one of my mum's many amazingly addictive inventions, which my family never bores of as she varies them, upgrades them and always serves it to us on the right occasion with exactly the right main course and pudding.

I have to say, most mums are 'the best' at everything and especially at cooking, but mine somehow manages three children, being a journalist, jogging, partying, travelling all over the world and anything else that includes action, hard work and fun. But, above all, she hosts the most amazing dinner parties, coordinated in such a way that you would have no idea about the organization behind them, as she is so laid-back. She gives me recipes that look unbelievably complicated to cook, and I freak, until I watch her and listen to her explain. It usually turns out to be easier than making a bowl of cornflakes and a cup of tea when you are not even hungover!

400g unsalted butter
pinch of ground mace
pinch of freshly grated nutmeg
⅓ teaspoon cayenne pepper
90g crabmeat **per person** (use both brown and white crabmeat but keep them separate, and make sure the crab is fresh and cooked! A good fishmonger will pick the crab for you and divide the meat into light and dark)
squeeze of lemon juice
salt and pepper

• Melt 240g of the butter gently, then pour it carefully into another pan, leaving behind the milky, curd-like solids.

• Add the spices and just the white crabmeat to the spiced butter. Mix well and taste. It shouldn't be too spicy from the cayenne, just subtle, not full-scale heat! Adjust accordingly, then add salt and pepper and a squeeze of lemon juice to taste.

• Boil the kettle. Meanwhile, fill each ramekin with a layer of the buttered white crab meat, followed by a layer of the untouched brown meat. Finish with a layer of the spicy white meat. You should just have enough room left at the top of the ramekins for the final layer, which is of clarified butter and which will be added **after the crab has been poached**.

• To poach the ramekins, place them in a roasting tin, pour in enough boiling water to come halfway up the **outside** of the ramekins – not in them – and place the tin in a preheated oven, 150°C/300°F/Gas 2. The hot water will

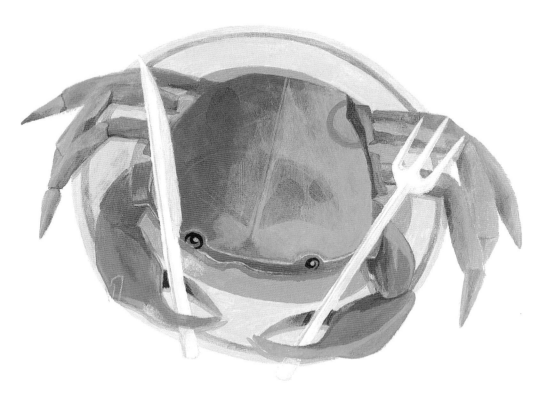

slowly cook the crab by heating up the ramekins.
• Cook for 25 minutes. Remove, cool, then clarify the rest of the butter and pour over each ramekin, like sealing wax. Place in the fridge to chill.
• Remove the ramekins from the fridge 20 minutes before you make your toast, so that they are cold, but not fridge cold. Then slip a slim knife blade all the way around the sides of each ramekin right to the bottom. Turn them out on to the palm of your hand and put each one,

butter side up, on individual plates. I usually leave them in the ramekin and give everyone a teaspoon – it's much easier and less fiddly!

Cannellini Beans with Garlic, Sage and Olive Oil

Serves 4

Remember, the beans need to be soaked for at least 8 hours so allow time to do this the night before.
Adding chopped tomatoes is optional.

240g dried cannellini beans, soaked (these need to soak for at least 8 hours in a pudding bowl. You may have to add more water from time to time to keep the beans covered)

a few sprigs of fresh rosemary and fresh sage

1 onion, roughly chopped

2 sticks celery, roughly chopped

4 cloves garlic, 2 left unpeeled

3 tablespoons olive oil, plus extra to serve

3 fresh tomatoes or 425g tin chopped tomatoes, seeded (optional)

salt and pepper

• Drain the soaked beans. Cook the beans in plenty of fresh water with a few sprigs of rosemary and sage, the onion and celery and 2 of the garlic cloves, peeled and halved. Cooking time will vary depending how old the beans are – cook until tender, but for at least one hour. Drain the water off, **but keep it** and discard the other vegetables.

• Sauté another sprig of fresh sage in the olive oil with 2 bruised cloves of garlic (see Tip). When the garlic begins to frizzle, remove it. Add the tomatoes, if you are using them – I would, as they add juice and flavour.

• Add the cooked beans. Turn the beans in the oil, then pour over enough of the reserved bean cooking water to cover the base of the saucepan. Season with salt and pepper – never season dried beans with salt during the initial cooking

stage, it will toughen the skins to husks – and cook until most of the liquid has evaporated.

• Transfer to an earthenware dish (if you have one) and let them cool. This dish is best eaten warm with a glug of olive oil poured over before serving. For a light lunch, serve with a tomato and mozzarella salad, and ciabatta bread.

Tip: Where a recipe calls for bruised cloves of garlic, it means that you don't take the skin off, you just crush the clove slightly but still leave it whole.

Poached Salmon

Serves 4

No, not stolen from a nearby river!

1 whole (approx 2 kg) salmon or sea trout
3 tablespoons olive oil
125ml (one glass) white wine
2 bulbs fennel
a large bunch of parsley
salt and pepper

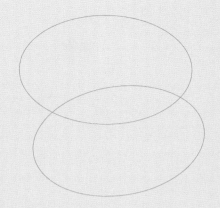

• Put a large piece of foil (enough to make into a parcel around the salmon later) on a baking sheet and lay the salmon on it.

Fold up the edges of the foil (to avoid spillage) spoon the olive oil over the fish and pour in the white wine.

Stuff the tummy with as much fennel as you can fit in, plus the parsley and salt and pepper.

Seal it all into a baggy parcel and cook at a very low temperature of 150°C/300°F/Gas 2 so that the fish retains its moisture and colour. (Fish is very easy to overcook, and not worth it if you have spent your rent on a nifty dinner.)

Cook for 1 hour.

Cool the fish in the foil until it is tepid. You will see a line down the fish (from the scales)... gently cut down this line with the sharp point of a knife, and you will be able to peel the skin back.

Serve with my potato salad, lemon and home-made mayonaise.

Tip: Farmed salmon are tasteless, so it is worth splashing out a bit. Buy the fish gutted but on the bone. You can have the head removed if you are squeamish! and ask the fishmonger to scale it for you. Do not buy a smaller fish – buy a big one and then you can make salmon fishcakes, or salmon and home-made mayonaise sandwiches later with the leftovers.

Sandwiches

The food you buy while at uni will be anything that takes your fancy in the supermarket when your student loan first comes in, and then after that you are guaranteed to get lazy. Cooking everyday will become a hassle and you will know how your mum felt every evening when you came home from school and slobbed in front of the TV waiting for supper! I don't recommend you buy microwave meals – just cook some bits and pieces on your days off and put them in the freezer, they'll taste much nicer and will cost a lot less.

When you really can't be bothered with making anything more than a sandwich, the following recipes are for when you get bored of cheese and tomato, ham and tomato, cucumber and tuna. Here are a few, Prêt a Manger-style!

Steak Sandwich

Serves 2

You can make this if good old mum comes to visit and brings you some goodies or if you raid the freezer before going back to uni!

50g butter

squeeze of lemon juice

2 tablespoons chopped fresh parsley

1 clove garlic, peeled and crushed to a paste with a little salt and pepper

1 teaspoon Dijon mustard (although any mustard is good with beef)

2 x 200g pieces of rump steak, about 1cm thick

dash of olive oil

2 small baguettes

salt and pepper

• Mash together the butter, lemon juice, parsley, garlic and mustard.

• Rub both sides of the steaks with olive oil and a little black pepper.

• Warm the bread in the oven. Grill the steaks for a couple of minutes on each side. If they are thicker than 1cm, grill for a little longer. Season them with some salt while they are cooking.

• Spread the butter mixture on the bread, and put any remaining butter mixture on the steaks while they are cooking. Sandwich the steaks while still hot and eat.

Hot Mozzarella Focaccia

Serves 4

Focaccia is an Italian bread which you can get in delis or Marks and Spencers or Sainsbury's.

350g buffalo mozzarella cheese or 'mozzarella di buffula' (drain off the preserving water, so that you have just the mozzarella balls)

100ml extra virgin olive oil

handful of fresh basil leaves (buy a plant in Sainsbury's to keep on the window sill)

2 bottled red chillies, thinly sliced

4 spring onions

loaf of focaccia bread

6 large thin slices of parma ham

2 tablespoons finely grated Parmesan cheese

black pepper

• Cut the mozzarella into thin slices and put in a shallow dish. Cover with olive oil, the basil leaves, which need to be torn with your hands a little, and the red chillies. Grind black pepper over this and cover with clingfilm. Leave to marinate for about 30 minutes.

• Meanwhile, grill the spring onions till slightly blackened in patches.

• Slice the focaccia in half horizontally and lay the two pieces cut sides up. Holding the cheese back, tip the bowl and pour the marinating oil and juices over the cut sides of the bread.

• Cover the bottom half of the bread with the Parma ham, the mozzarella and the remaining bits in the bowl, then the grilled onions. Finally, add the grated Parmesan.

• Top with the other half of bread and put on a preheated baking sheet. Whack in a preheated oven, 180°C/350°F/Gas 4, for 20–25 minutes, till the cheese oozes out.

Spiced Indian Chicken Sandwich

Makes 2 large sandwiches

Just halve the recipe if you can't be bothered to make the other one that will be inevitably stolen by someone else in the kitchen!

8 large free-range chicken wings

olive oil, for frying

2 small red hot chillies, seeded and finely chopped **(don't rub your eyes or lick your fingers – it's punishing!)**

3 spring onions, chopped

2 cloves garlic, peeled and crushed to a paste with a little salt and pepper

1 knife point of ground turmeric (if you can find it amid jars of random dried herbs or in someone else's cupboard!)

2 small crusty baguettes or large baps

pinch of sugar

juice of 1 lemon

salt and pepper

butter and mayonnaise, to serve

• Salt and pepper the chicken wings.

• Heat enough oil to cover the bottom of a shallow frying pan, add the seasoned chicken. As soon as one side of the wings has coloured a little, turn them over and cook the other side for 2–3 minutes. Turn down the heat, partly cover with a lid and leave over a moderate heat for about 30 minutes or until the wings are cooked right through. You may add more oil from time to time if necessary.

• Lift the chicken wings out on to kitchen paper to drain. Keep the pan with everything in. When cool enough to handle, take the meat off the bones – it should fall away easily; set aside.

• Mash the chopped chillies, spring onions, crushed garlic and turmeric to a paste. A pestle and mortar is good for this. Use a few drops of olive oil, too, to make it easier to mash.

• Split the bread in half and toast the cut sides.

• Cook the spice paste in the pan that the chicken was cooked in. Use a little more oil if need be, but **do not let it burn**.

• Return the chicken to the pan, coat it in the spice paste, season and add the sugar and lemon juice. Slather the toasted bread with butter and mayonnaise, pile on the hot chicken and scoff the lot!

Sauces to Save the Day

If I was to find one reason why English food is good, it's because we have a sauce to go with everything. I think it originates from olden times when there were no fridges, so a sauce was needed to cover the taste of meat that was going bad. They're just as useful now if you are a drunken student and you find something dodgy in the fridge. Just whack on some HP sauce, or make a sauce and keep it in the fridge, but for no longer than a week please!

Sauces can be put on anything. Some sweet ones go well with meat, like orange sauce with duck or apple sauce and pork. They're quick and easy to make, you can reheat them, and they taste good.

Cumberland Sauce

This is ideal with pork, duck and even goose!

2 oranges
225g redcurrant jelly
1 teaspoon Dijon mustard
75ml port
pinch of ground ginger
salt and pepper

• Peel the oranges thinly, then squeeze the oranges to extract the juice. Cut the orange peel into matchstick strips. Place in a saucepan, cover with cold water and bring to the boil for 2 minutes. Drain.
• Heat the jelly and mustard together over a low heat, whisking them to a smooth consistency. Add the juice of the cranges and the port, with a good grinding of black pepper and a pinch of salt and ginger to taste.
• Stir in the orange peel then simmer for 5 minutes. Pour into a glass dish or jar and leave to cool. If covered and stored in the fridge this sauce will keep for weeks.

Apple Sauce

If you use ordinary apples instead of cooking apples, just cancel out the sugar. Apple sauce is addictive, so make plenty of it!

50g butter
450g cooking apples, washed and roughly chopped
1 tablespoon brown sugar
3 cloves (optional)
juice of ½ lemon

• Put all the ingredients in a heavy-bottomed saucepan. Cover and cook over a medium heat for 10–15 minutes, or until the apples are a soft collapsed heap. Remember to lift the lid occasionally and stir to stop them from sticking.
• Pass the mixture through a sieve to get rid of the pips, core and skin and then blend to a purée in a food processor.
• Taste, as the sauce might need more sugar. If it is too runny, then boil it down, but not too furiously as it will burn and you will be pretty annoyed! If it is too stiff, add some butter and a dash of water.

Bread Sauce

For 10 people, so halve it if you aren't feeding the five thousand!

30g butter

1 onion, finely chopped

800ml full-fat milk (this should come one-quarter to halfway up your saucepan, but you may need to keep adding more, so don't use the last of it in a cup of tea or on a bowl of cornflakes!)

1 bay leaf (optional)

150g breadcrumbs (make by putting sliced bread in a blender; stale bread is best, which is always easy to find in a student kitchen!)

freshly grated nutmeg

salt and pepper

• Make this sauce early and then reheat it when the roast is cooked, adding a little more milk, so it's not too thick and stodgy.

• Melt the butter in a pan and add the onion – 20 seconds of sautéing will do, then add the milk, bay leaf and a pinch of salt, and bring to the boil. Do not actually let it boil; just as it reaches boiling point remove the pan from the heat, cover and let it cool, so the flavours can infuse the milk.

• Then, over a low heat, stir in the breadcrumbs. Usually I have to add a bit more milk at this stage – you can tell if it's too thick as it gets doughy and hard to stir, you want it to have a porridge-like texture. Cook for 15 minutes.

• While it is cooking grate in some nutmeg and stir in some freshly ground pepper.

• This sauce is best eaten with roast chicken or turkey.

Green Sauce

This sauce goes really well with halibut or any other large chunky fish like swordfish. I cooked it for my headmaster and his wife, as cooking for dinner parties was one of the ways I raised money for my gap year.

2 tablespoons of capers, finely chopped (rinse thoroughly if preserved in brine)

6–7 cournichons (little pickled gherkins), finely chopped

2 tablespoons of flat leaf parsley, finely chopped

2 tablespoons of curly leaf parsley, finely chopped

2 tablespoons coriander, finely chopped

6 cloves of garlic, chopped and mashed

1 hard boiled egg, finely chopped

2 tablespoons mint, finely chopped

1 tablespoon dill, finely chopped

1 tablespoon chervil (if you can find it)

12 anchovies removed from oil and finely chopped

olive oil

salt and pepper

• Put the garlic, anchovies, capers and all the herbs into a bowl.

• Dribble in some olive oil – very gradually, as you ony want it moist enough to stick together.

• Stir in the egg and cournichons, and it is ready to serve with freshly pan fried fish!

Cranberry Sauce

This is particularly good with cold turkey sandwiches on Boxing Day.

500g fresh cranberries
grated zest and juice of 1 orange
225g sugar
30g butter
1 tablespoon Grand Marnier (optional)
100ml water

• Put the cranberries, zest and juice of the orange, sugar, butter and Grand Marnier (if using) in a saucepan.
• Add the water and bring to the boil. After a minute or so of fierce bubbling, lower the heat to a simmer and cook for 10 minutes, until the berries have popped. You may need to add a bit more water so the berries don't stick and burn.
• You will end up with a thick and fruity sauce. Taste it in case you need more sugar, then tip into a bowl and cool before serving.

Brandy Butter

Ideal with Christmas pudding!

150g unsalted butter (**needs to be soft,** but don't microwave it, as it will melt and burn)
225g icing sugar, sifted
50g ground almonds
3 tablespoons brandy

• Beat the butter until soft. You will have to mash and pound it.
• Add the sifted icing sugar and beat together until pale and creamy.
• Mix in the ground almonds and when smooth add the brandy. Add 1 tablespoon first and mix well, then taste to see if more is needed – obviously it will be!

Mars Bar Sauce

I have found there are three types of chocolate lovers: those who like sweet chocolate, those who like it amazingly dark and bitter, and the legendary chocoholics who never turn down any type of chocolate, whether it's melted in a pocket and covered in fluff or is the last one left in the box with some rank filling inside!
This sauce will satisfy any sweet tooth and is so easy to make.

4 king-size Mars bars or 6 normal sized ones, cut into chunks
1 tablespoon cream (optional)

• Place the Mars bars chunks in a heavy-bottomed saucepan and melt slowly and patiently over the lowest heat possible. No tasting is a safe piece of advice, otherwise there'll be none left!
• If you have some cream, add a tablespoon once the chocolate has melted and stir in.

Richest Chocolate Sauce in the World

This is a much-loved family recipe.

1 bar good-quality (70% cocoa solids) chocolate (or 2 bars depending on the greed factor and if you have convinced yourself it is worth sharing with friends!), broken into pieces
1 tablespoon water
15g butter
2 generous tablespoons double cream
3 generous tablespoons golden syrup

• Melt the chocolate with the water and butter in a saucepan, over a really low heat.
• When melted, add the cream and golden syrup and stir until melted.
• Serve with bananas, ice cream or whatever… or eat it straight off the spoon!

Cakes, Biscuits and Puddings

If you are like me, you will get withdrawal symptoms from your mum's puddings so this section is just in case you feel the need to bake!

Most baking is a piece of cake, not trying to be corny! You just mix up some basics like eggs, sugar and flour and throw it in the oven.

Shortcrust Pastry
Makes a 20cm pastry case

175g plain white or wholemeal flour
pinch of salt
85g butter, chilled
3 tablespoons cold water

• Sift the flour and salt into a bowl, and grate the butter, straight from the fridge, into the flour.
• Using your fingertips, rub in the butter with minimum handling – **you don't want the butter to melt**. Add 2 tablespoons water, little by little, just enough to bind the mixture together. Wrap the pastry in clingfilm and chill in the fridge for at least 20 minutes.
• Roll out the pastry on a lightly floured surface to fit a 20cm tart tin.
• To bake the pastry blind, cut a circle of greaseproof paper the same size as the base of the pastry case and lay over the pastry. Place a handful of dried beans on top of the paper – these prevent the pastry rising.
• Put the pastry case in a preheated oven, 180°C/350°F/Gas 4, and bake for 10–15 minutes. Then remove the beans and paper and bake for a further 5–10 minutes.

Sweet Pastry
Makes a 20cm pastry case

225g plain white flour
175g butter, softened, cut into pieces
65g caster sugar
2 egg yolks

• Sift the flour into a bowl and make a 'well' in the middle.
• Put the butter, sugar and egg yolks in the 'well'.
• Using your fingers, work quickly and lightly to incorporate the flour and make a dough – pastry doesn't agree with too much handling. Wrap the pastry in clingfilm and chill for 30 minutes.
• Roll out the pastry on a lightly floured surface to line a 20cm dish, then chill for another 20–30 minutes.
• Tear off a bit of greaseproof paper and place it over the pastry. Cover with dried beans.
• Cook in a preheated oven, 180°C/350°F/Gas 4 for 15–20 minutes. Then remove the beans and prick the base and cook for another 10 minutes.

Special Chocolate Cake – the one I make!

Serves 5

This recipe is dedicated to my little sister Charissa who cooked this cake for my mum and managed to burn it to a crisp – so don't forget to set the timer!

175g plain chocolate, broken into pieces
175g unsalted butter, softened
75g caster sugar
4 eggs, separated
90g ground almonds
90g plain flour, sifted

For the chocolate fudge icing:
125ml milk
90g sugar
125g plain chocolate, broken into pieces
45g butter

• To make the cake, put the chocolate in a heat-proof bowl. Stand the bowl over a pan of simmering water until it melts. **Never melt chocolate directly in a pan as it goes grainy**. Stir well.
• Cream the butter and sugar together until frothy. Beat in the egg yolks bit by bit. Add the melted chocolate and the ground almonds.
• Whisk the egg whites in a big clean bowl until soft peaks form. Do not go on beating or they will collapse. Using a metal tablespoon, gently fold some egg white and some flour into the mixture, until it has all been used.
• Spread the cake mixture evenly into two greased 17cm sandwich tins. Bake at 150°C/300°F/Gas 2 for 20 minutes. Test with a skewer

– there will be no mixture on it if it is ready.
• Remove the tins from the oven. Leave for a few minutes then slip a knife around the edges of the tins and turn the cakes out on to a wire rack.
• To make the icing, bring the milk and sugar to the boil and stir for 5 minutes. Take the pan off the heat and stir in the chocolate and the butter until both have melted. Pour the icing into a bowl. When cool put in the fridge and it will thicken as it cools – **this makes it easier to spread**. Spread half on top of one cake. Sandwich the other cake on top then cover with the rest of the icing.

Brownies
Makes 8–10

110g plain chocolate, broken into pieces
110g butter
225g caster sugar
2 eggs, beaten
110g plain flour, sifted
½ teaspoon baking powder
110g chopped walnuts
pinch of salt

Chocolate Chip Cookies
Makes 30

160g unsalted butter, softened
85g light soft brown sugar
85g caster sugar
2 eggs, beaten
400g plain flour
½ teaspoon bicarbonate of soda
½ teaspoon baking powder
¼ teaspoon salt
200g semi-sweet chocolate pieces (I usually use a bar of bitter chocolate or of Cadbury's and roughly chop it into Smartie-sized chunks – about 5mm)

• Put the chocolate and butter in a heatproof bowl. Stand the bowl over a saucepan of gently simmering water until it melts.
• When melted, take the bowl off the heat and stir in all the other ingredients.
• Spread the mixture into a greased, 18 x 28cm shallow baking tin and bake in a preheated oven, 180°C/350°F/Gas 4, for 30 minutes.
• If you can resist, let the mixture cool in the tin for 10 minutes – it will sink a little bit. Then cut the brownies into 8–10 'squares' and cool on a wire rack.

• Cream the butter and both sugars in a blender or with a wooden spoon until light and fluffy.
• Add the eggs, one at a time, waiting until the first is completely incorporated before adding the second, to avoid the mixture curdling.
• Sift together the flour, bicarbonate, baking powder and salt. Fold into the mixture, add the chocolate chips and stir well with a wooden spoon. You should have a stiff doughy mixture.
• Roll walnut-sized pieces of dough between your palms and put them on two greased baking sheets. Leave a space between each cookie – do not cram them on as they need space to expand.
• Cook in a preheated oven, 180°C/350°F/Gas 4, for 15–20 minutes or until the edges are firm but the centre is still slightly gooey. Remove and let cool. Store in a cookie jar for up to five days.

Fridge Cake

Serves 5

This recipe was the pig-out cake in our day room at school, which my partner in crime Al Berks used to make. No oven is required, just a fridge, which is probably even scarier due to the fact that fridges rarely get cleaned. So, please make sure that you have at least one clean shelf and it doesn't stink too much!

175g digestive biscuits
90g margarine
30g sugar
60g golden syrup
2 tablespoons cocoa powder
60g nuts, roughly chopped
30g glacé cherries, roughly chopped

For the topping:
30g margarine
1 tablespoon cocoa powder
115g icing sugar

• Crush the biscuits to fine crumbs, either by whizzing them in a food processor or by putting them in a plastic bag and crushing them with a rolling pin.
• Melt the margarine, sugar and golden syrup in a saucepan over a low heat. When liquid, stir in the cocoa powder, biscuit crumbs, half the nuts and the chopped cherries.
• Put the mixture into an 18cm cake tin and press down well. Leave to cool in the fridge.
• To make the topping, melt the margarine and add the cocoa and icing sugar. Add a dash of water if it looks a bit dry. Spread over the cold cake mixture and sprinkle the rest of the nuts on top. Return to the fridge and serve chilled.

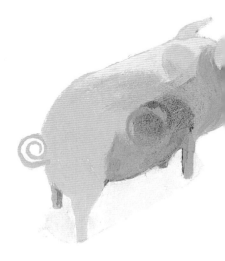

Helen's Mad Birthday Cake

Serves 5

Helen used to bake this for me every birthday, and I'd bake my chocolate one (see page 112) for her. It was the coolest cake ever, and every year it had a new surprise on top. This cake is yummy, but can make you feel like you're at one of those birthday parties when you were little and your eyes were bigger than your stomach. There was always one child who went green and was sick playing musical bumps!

112g butter

112g caster sugar

1 teaspoon vanilla essence (if you want the cake to be chocolaty add 50g cocoa powder)

2 eggs

112g self raising flour, sifted

For the frosting and topping:

112g butter

225g icing sugar, sifted (Helen uses 112g icing sugar and 112g of caster to give it some texture)

1 teaspoon vanilla essence

selection of chocolate bars (I recommend Flake, Maltesers, Smarties, Crunchie, Caramel, Minstrels)

• Cream the butter and sugar together in a blender or by hand in a mixing bowl until light and fluffy.

• Add the vanilla essence (and cocoa powder if using). Beat in the eggs, one by one, and then fold in the flour.

• Pour the mixture into two shallow cake tins or one deep one and bake at 180°C/350°F/Gas 4 for 25–30 minutes.

• When the cake is ready, take it out and let it cool. If it is one big cake then slice it in half horizontally so you have two round halves.

• To make the topping, cream together the butter, sugar and vanilla essence until fluffy.

Using half the icing, spread a layer on one of the cakes then crumble over some Cadbury's Flake. Sandwich the two cakes together.

• Spread the remaining icing on the top of the cake. Decorate with Maltesers around the edge, then giant Smarties and whatever else you have chopped up.

Flapjacks

Makes 24

These are easy to cook and last for days. Funnily enough, I had never really enjoyed them until a great friend Vanessa brought them on our first Duke of Edinburgh trek. From then on, they became a strict tradition. They are full of oats, a slow-release energy ingredient for the sporty ones out there, and always nice to nibble on.

75g butter or margarine
2–3 tablespoons golden syrup
75g soft brown sugar
150g rolled oats/porridge oats or muesli

• Melt the butter or margarine, golden syrup and soft brown sugar, in a medium-sized saucepan over a low heat. Stir as the mixture melts and don't let it burn.
• When the mixture has melted and combined, stir in the oats, a little at a time, until the mixture is sticky and the oats are coated.
• Press the mixture into a greased 18 x 28cm shallow baking tin.
• Bake at 160°C/325°F/Gas 3 for 15–20 minutes until golden and set. Cut into 'squares'. The flapjacks are not crisp until cold, so don't worry – just be patient. I personally can't be, as they are great crumbly and hot!.

Tip: You can use caster sugar instead of soft brown sugar, as I did in the Cloud Forest, when I made these as snacks to eat after we had been digging banana plant holes!

Cheese Jacks

Makes 12

Something savoury to nibble on.

150g porridge oats
175g Cheddar cheese, grated
1 egg, beaten
50g butter or margarine
½ teaspoon crushed dried rosemary (if you have it)
salt and pepper

• Mix all the ingredients together well.
• Press into a shallow square cake tin and bake in a preheated oven, 180°C/350°F/Gas 4, for about 40 minutes until golden.
• Cut into slices and serve hot or cold.

Banana Bread

Serves 4–6

225g self-raising flour
¾ level teaspoon ground mixed spice (optional)
½ teaspoon salt
100g caster sugar
100g butter, cut into small pieces
1 tablespoon honey
100g sultanas
450g ripe bananas, peeled and mashed with a fork
2 eggs
juice of 1 lemon

• Sift the flour, mixed spice (if you have), salt and sugar into a bowl. Add the butter.
• Beat in all the remaining ingredients, then pour the mixture into a greased 23cm loaf tin.
• Bake in a preheated oven, 180°C/350°F/Gas 4, for 1 hour, then for a further 30 minutes at 170°C/330°F/Gas 3½. Take out of the oven and leave cool in the tin before turning out the banana bread.

Carrot Cake

Serves 5

2 eggs
100g raw brown sugar
75ml oil
100g self-raising flour, sifted
1 teaspoon ground cinnamon
½ teaspoon ground nutmeg
175g carrots, peeled and finely grated
50g desiccated coconut (optional)
50g raisins

For the icing:
130g unsalted butter, softened
300g full-fat soft cheese (Philadelphia), softened
160g icing sugar, sifted

• Grease an 18cm cake tin then line with grease-proof paper. Whisk the eggs and sugar together until creamy.
• Slowly whisk in the oil, then add the remaining ingredients and mix together evenly.
• Pour the mixture into the prepared cake tin. Level the surface and bake in a preheated oven, 190°C/375°F/Gas 5, for 20–25 minutes, until firm to the touch and golden brown. Turn out and cool on a wire rack.
• Beat all the icing ingredients together to make a thick cream and spread over the cooled cake.
• **Refrigerate the cake for 2 hours before serving**… yeah right 2 hours, but try to attempt it – for the cake's sake not yours! All cooking instructions and rules are there for a reason, even if some are there to be broken!

Queen's Pudding

Serves 5

butter, for greasing

75g fresh breadcrumbs (the crusts removed and the bread blended to crumbs in a food processor)

grated zest of 1 lemon

300ml single cream

300ml milk

50g butter

3 eggs, separated

150g caster sugar

4 rounded tablespoons jam (strawberry, raspberry, apricot – whatever you have)

• Rub a baking dish with a little butter and put the breadcrumbs in the dish.

• Put the lemon rind, cream, milk and butter in a saucepan and heat until just warm.

• In a mixing bowl beat the egg yolks lightly together with half of the caster sugar. Gradually stir in the heated milk. Pour this mixture over the breadcrumbs, and bake in the centre of a preheated oven, 180°C/375°F/Gas 4, for about 25 minutes or until set – when wobbled, the dish should show that the pudding is no longer liquid.

• Remove from the oven and spread the jam over the top.

• Whisk the egg whites in a clean bowl till stiff. **Fold** in the remaining sugar. Pile this meringue over the jam and return to the oven for another 15 minutes until golden and crisp.

Drop Scones

Serves 5

Easy, yummy and cheap to make.

100g self-raising flour, sifted

25g sugar

1 free-range egg

120ml milk

butter, for greasing the pan

• Beat all the ingredients together in a mixing bowl. The mixture should be fairly thick.

• Heat a frying pan over a medium heat. Brush lightly with butter, and drop tablespoons of the mixture into the pan, 1–2 at a time. Leave until bubbles surface on the mixture and a skin starts to form. Turn carefully with a palette knife and cook until golden brown on the other side.

Lemon Meringue Pie

Serves 6

uncooked 20cm shortcrust pastry case, chilled
(see page 111)
beaten egg white, for brushing

For the lemon filling:
grated zest and juice of 3 lemons
45g cornflour
300ml water
3 egg yolks
80g vanilla caster sugar
60g unsalted butter, cut into small pieces

For the meringue:
3 egg whites
120g vanilla caster sugar

• Bake the pastry blind in a preheated oven, 190°C/375°F/Gas 5, for 15 minutes (that is, with dried beans on top – see page 111). Remove the beans, brush the pastry with a little beaten egg white and return to the oven for 5 minutes. Remove the pastry case from the oven and turn the heat down to 180°C/350°F/Gas 4.

• Meanwhile, make the filling. Put the lemon zest and juice in a heatproof bowl set over a saucepan of simmering water **(the water must not touch the bottom of the bowl)**. Add the cornflour and whisk in 2 tablespoons of the water until you have a smooth paste.

• Bring the remaining water to the boil in another pan, then whisk it into the lemon mixture until it is thick and bubbling.

• Remove from the heat and whisk in the egg yolks, sugar and butter. Leave to cool slightly while you make the meringue.

• Whisk the egg whites in a clean bowl until stiff. Scatter in one-third of the sugar and whisk again. Fold in another third with a **metal spoon**.

• Spread the lemon mixture over the pastry case. Pile the meringue on top and sprinkle it with the remaining sugar. Bake for 15–20 minutes. Take out when the meringue is golden and the top is hard. Serve with cream.

Lemon Cheesecake
Serves 5

175g ginger biscuits or digestives
75g butter
grated chocolate, to decorate

For the lemon cheese:
225g cream cheese
2–3 tablespoons milk
grated zest and juice of 1 lemon
1 tablespoon caster sugar

• Crush the biscuits to fine crumbs, either by whizzing them in a food processor or by putting them in a plastic bag and crushing them with a rolling pin.
• Melt the butter in a saucepan over a low heat. Add the biscuit crumbs and stir well. Press the mixture firmly and evenly into a greased 20cm flan tin. Refrigerate until chilled – the biscuit base hardens as it chills.
• Put the cream cheese in a bowl and beat with a wooden spoon till soft. Add the milk, a little at a time, beating well to make a smooth mixture. Quickly stir in the lemon rind and juice and the caster sugar.
• When the mixture is smooth, pour over the biscuit base and level with a knife. Cover with foil and put in the fridge to chill for at least 3 hours.
• When the cheesecake is set, grate some chocolate over the top to decorate.

Lemon and Orange Fromage
Serves 5

grated zest and juice of 1 lemon
grated zest and juice of 1 orange
15g gelatine
284ml carton double cream
2 eggs, separated
50g caster sugar

• Put the lemon and orange juices in a small heatproof bowl and sprinkle over the gelatine. Leave to soften for about 5 minutes, then stand the bowl in a saucepan of barely simmering water and heat until the gelatine has dissolved.
• Meanwhile, whip the cream until stiff.
• In another clean bowl, whisk the egg whites until they are stiff.
• Beat the egg yolks with the sugar and the lemon and orange zests, then stir in the dissolved gelatine mixture. Carefully fold in the whipped cream, followed by the stiff egg whites.
• Divide the mixture between individual serving dishes and chill for 1 hour before serving.

Tasmanian Lemon Pudding

Serves 5

125g butter, softened
275g vanilla caster sugar
4 eggs, separated
4 tablespoons plain flour, sifted
400ml milk
grated zest and juice of 2 lemons

• Cream the butter with the vanilla caster sugar
until light and fluffy.
• Beat in the egg yolks, then the flour and milk,
a little at a time. Add the grated zest and juice of
the lemons.
• Whisk the egg whites **in a clean grease-free
bowl** until stiff and add them to the mixture,
folding lightly with a metal spoon as usual, to
incorporate air into the mixture.
• Pour the mixture into a greased baking dish so
that it comes about 5cm up the side of the dish.
Cook in a preheated oven, 180°C/350°F/Gas 4,
for about 25–30 minutes, until slightly brown on
top and obviously set faintly shuddery.

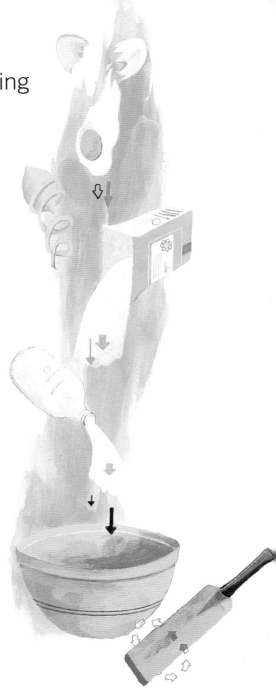

Hot Banana and Rum Soufflé

Serves 2

1 large banana, peeled and roughly chopped

1 teaspoon lemon juice

1 tablespoon single cream

20g brown sugar

1 teaspoon dark rum

1 egg, separated

7g self-raising flour

• Place the chopped banana in a blender with the lemon juice, cream, brown sugar, rum and egg yolk. Blend together, then add the flour. Blend again, then transfer to a bowl.

• Place the egg white in a clean, grease-free bowl and whisk until stiff. Fold gently into the banana mixture with a metal spoon.

• Pour the mixture into two individual greased ramekin dishes and bake in the centre of a preheated oven, 180°C/350°F/Gas 4, for 20–25 minutes or until well risen.

• Serve immediately.

Fruit Crumble

Serves 4

You can use almost any fruit, for example apples, peaches, pears, apricots, pineapple and banana.

2 apples and 2 pears, peeled and sliced into chunks

50–75g sugar, to taste (I use brown muscovado and caster sugar mixed)

For the crumble:

150g plain flour

100g butter

1 tablespoon water

75g sugar

• Put the fruit in a greased baking dish. Add sugar according to how much you like and how sour the fruit is.

• To make the crumble, whizz the flour and butter together in a food processor or rub the mixture with your fingers until it resembles breadcrumbs. Sprinkle with the water and stir lightly with a fork. Stir in the sugar.

• Cover the fruit with the crumble mix until you can't see the fruit. Bake in a preheated oven, 200°C/400°F/Gas 6, for 35 minutes or until the top is crisp and golden. Serve hot.

Notes

Index of recipes